The Pickoff

The Pickoff

*Coaching Christians
to Safely Round the Bases*

T. SCOTT WOMBLE

WIPF & STOCK · Eugene, Oregon

THE PICKOFF
Coaching Christians to Safely Round the Bases

Copyright © 2025 T. Scott Womble. All rights reserved. Except for brief quotations in critical publications or reviews, no part of this book may be reproduced in any manner without prior written permission from the publisher. Write: Permissions, Wipf and Stock Publishers, 199 W. 8th Ave., Suite 3, Eugene, OR 97401.

Wipf & Stock
An Imprint of Wipf and Stock Publishers
199 W. 8th Ave., Suite 3
Eugene, OR 97401

www.wipfandstock.com

PAPERBACK ISBN: 979-8-3852-4249-8
HARDCOVER ISBN: 979-8-3852-4250-4
EBOOK ISBN: 979-8-3852-4251-1

Scripture quotations taken from the (NASB®) New American Standard Bible®, Copyright © 1995, 2020 by The Lockman Foundation. Used by permission. All rights reserved. lockman.org

*For those who will follow after Christ.
May you circle the bases and reach home safely.*

Contents

Acknowledgments ix
Introduction xi

Part 1—Erased on the Bases
Chapter 1: The Art of Deception 3
Chapter 2: Quick Feet 20
Chapter 3: Caught Sleeping 28
Chapter 4: Caught Leaning 42
Chapter 5: Bad Advice 54
Chapter 6: Imposing One's Will 69

Part 2—Circling the Bases
Chapter 7: Successful Baserunning 81
Chapter 8: The Necessity of Having Fun 90

Part 3—Extra Innings
Chapter 9: The Danger of Standing Still 101
Chapter 10: Not a Game 106

Conclusion 117

Endnotes 121
Appendixes 133
Bibliography 149
Scripture Index 153

Acknowledgments

ONE OF MY ALL-TIME favorite books is *The Screwtape Letters* by C. S. Lewis. This 1942 classic is about a senior demon named Screwtape who writes letters to his nephew Wormwood, a junior demon. Screwtape mentors his nephew with the goal of guiding a Christian (called "The Patient") away from our Lord, and toward Satan.

As one will see in this book, Lewis's masterpiece has had a tremendous impact on me. While I write as a baseball coach assisting Christian baserunners, at times I imagine what the enemy is thinking and explore the various tactics he employs as he attempts to pick off runners. Such imagination must be attributed to Lewis. So, if you enjoy this book, and have yet to read *The Screwtape Letters*, you'll want to read that classic.

As warped as Screwtape is, I'll forever be thankful that he wrote his thirty-one letters. Not only do they provide insight into the demonic mind, but they put the Christian on high "alert." I'd like to thank him for showing his hand. While he certainly never imagined such, his antics have always served to remind me about the reality of spiritual forces among us.

I want to thank Dr. Mike Pabarcus, Matt Campbell, and Nathan Diveley for reading the book and providing me with general feedback. Besides being committed Jesus-followers, they love baseball and get the pickoff metaphor.

Also, I'm so grateful to Dr. Leonard Sweet and Dr. Don Sanders for providing recommendations for the book. Len was the

Acknowledgments

mentor for my doctoral program, and I'm in debt to him for his mentorship and continual help. Don is an old friend who understands my love for both Jesus and baseball.

And, of course, I'm in debt to my editors. I've been blessed to have Penny Shadow, Norma Baker, Rick Fordyce, and my wife Lisa, clean up the typos and poor grammar I left behind. They've made this readable and helped me bring this project to completion.

Introduction

THE 1974 WORLD SERIES featured the Oakland Athletics (A's) and the Los Angeles Dodgers. The A's were a powerhouse, having won the World Series in both '72 and '73—and they would go on to win this series as well. While the A's had edged out both the Reds and Mets four games to three in '72 and '73 respectively, they steamrolled the Dodgers four games to one.

The only bright spot for the Dodgers came in Game 2, a 3–2 victory at Dodger Stadium. Future Hall of Famer Don Sutton pitched eight shutout innings that day before allowing the first two batters to reach base in the top of the ninth inning. At that point, Dodger manager Walter Alston brought in his closer, Mike Marshall.

In 1974, Marshall pitched in 106 regular season games and racked up 208 1/3 innings pitched—all out of the bullpen! Those ridiculous numbers earned him the Cy Young Award. Putting these insane numbers aside, Marshall had a great pickoff move and he would soon display it.

After Marshall came in, he gave up a hit to Joe Rudi and two runs scored. With no outs and the Dodgers lead shrinking to 3–2, the game was heating up. Marshall proceeded to strike out Gene Tenace. With one out and the tying run on first, the A's sent in speedster Herb Washington to run for Rudi. The A's hoped Washington could steal second base and get into scoring position.

Washington was a track star who held the indoor world record in both the 50 and 100-yard dash. As Washington stretched out his lead at first base, Marshall stepped off and faked a throw

INTRODUCTION

to first. After regrouping, Washington once again looked to get a good lead. In an attempt to keep Washington guessing and uncomfortable, Marshall stepped off the rubber. This happened yet a third time. During the fourth sequence, Marshall threw over and picked off the speedster.

I was only nine years-old, but Marshall's pickoff is forever etched in my mind. Oh, by the way, with the rally over, Marshall then struck out Angel Mangual to secure the lone Dodger victory.

To this day, I love watching pickoff attempts. Unfortunately, this cat and mouse game is becoming a lost aspect of baseball. With an emphasis on power over speed, fewer bases are being stolen than in years past. Consequently, it seems like fewer pitchers are taught the deceptive skills that make a great pickoff artist. To make things worse, Major League Baseball (MLB) made a rule change in 2023 that now only permits pitchers to make two pickoff attempts per at bat.

Having played and watched a lot of baseball, I've observed six primary reasons a player gets picked off, each of which is discussed in chapters 1–6. It's helpful to know that when discussing the pickoff in the context of this book, I'm always visualizing a runner being picked off at first base (not second or third base).

But this isn't really a book about baseball, it's about the church (the people of God). The pickoff serves as a metaphor that speaks of an enemy (demonic forces portrayed here as the pitcher) who tries to impede the progress of Christian baserunners. If we want to successfully make it to home plate, we must be aware of the enemy's arsenal of weapons working against the church.

Problematic is that the American church has become "user friendly" and seldom addresses the reality of spiritual warfare. In fact, we've come to the point where we readily toss aside biblical passages we find objectionable. Indeed, it is shocking how we hold our own intellect and sense of morality in such high esteem that they reign over God's word. Nevertheless, we would be wise to remember the Apostle Paul's words to the Ephesians, as they are crucial to the flourishing church. He said,

INTRODUCTION

¹⁰ Finally, be strong in the Lord and in the strength of His might. ¹¹ Put on the full armor of God, so that you will be able to stand firm against the schemes of the devil. ¹² For our struggle is not against flesh and blood, but against the rulers, against the powers, against the world forces of this darkness, against the spiritual forces of wickedness in the heavenly places. ¹³ Therefore, take up the full armor of God, so that you will be able to resist on the evil day, and having done everything, to stand firm. ¹⁴ Stand firm therefore, having belted your waist with truth, and having put on the breastplate of righteousness, ¹⁵ and having strapped on your feet the preparation of the gospel of peace; ¹⁶ in addition to all, taking up the shield of faith with which you will be able to extinguish all the flaming arrows of the evil one. ¹⁷ And take the helmet of salvation and the sword of the Spirit, which is the word of God. ¹⁸ With every prayer and request, pray at all times in the Spirit, and with this in view, be alert with all perseverance and every request for all the saints (Eph 6:10–18).

In life, as in baseball, we all require some coaching. And sound coaching goes beyond preparing your team to beat an opponent. Thus, chapters 7–8 address further keys to promoting baserunning success. After all, there is more to life than just avoiding mistakes!

Finally, in the section titled, "Extra Innings," chapter 9 briefly discusses how the enemy will pivot to another strategy if he can't pick off the runner. While the baseball metaphors are helpful, chapter 10 reminds us that being a Jesus-follower is no game. Because we are engaged in spiritual warfare, I briefly provide true war stories that drive home the seriousness of the situation.

In summary, this is a metaphorical look at how to coach Christian baserunners. So, if you're a Jesus-follower who is intent on helping others circle the bases, this is the book for you.

PART 1
Erased on the Bases

CHAPTER 1

The Art of Deception

STEVE CARLTON WAS ONE of the greatest pitchers of all-time. Carlton won four Cy Young awards as the National League's best pitcher, had 4,136 strikeouts (fourth all-time), and had 329 wins (eleventh all-time). He also had a filthy pickoff move to first base. In fact, his 146 pickoffs rank first all-time in MLB.

Carlton was left-handed, and when it comes to picking runners off first base, left-handed pitchers have a distinct advantage over their counterparts. This is because lefties who have mastered this craft, like Carlton, are able to straddle the line of what's legal and illegal, and thus, deceive the runner. Illegal movements are called "balks," and pitchers with great pickoff moves come dangerously close to balking. Some undoubtedly do balk but simply get away with it as this is a judgment-call violation.

There are thirteen illegal actions a pitcher can make that may result in a balk. If a balk occurs, the runners are allowed to advance one base. Of the thirteen movements, one is of specific interest, as left-handed pitchers make it difficult for both runners and umpires to detect this illegal action.

The key directive left-handed pitchers flirt with is Rule 8.05(c). It says, "The pitcher, while touching his plate (the rubber), fails to step directly toward a base before throwing to that base." The greatest pickoff artists make it appear as if they are throwing home, not to the base. Through this deception, they are able to

The Pickoff

pick off the runner. When throwing to first base, this deceptive move can only be done by left-handed pitchers.

This tactic is the primary means used to pick runners off first base. In fact, the seven pitchers with seventy-five career pickoffs, or more, are all left-handed.[1] And it's a safe bet they were all masters of deception. Interestingly, while deceiving the runner is not one of the thirteen illegal actions resulting in a balk, the comment of Rule 8.05(c) mentions that "an attempt to deceive the runner . . . shall be called a balk."[2]

There's another form of deception that sometimes results in a runner getting picked off base. It's an old playground scheme called "the hidden ball trick." This can be as simple as the first baseman huddling up with the pitcher and sticking the ball in his own glove. The key to this trick is making the runner believe that the pitcher has the ball.

Because a pitcher is not allowed to step on the rubber without the ball, runners are always taught to remain on the base until the pitcher first steps on the rubber. But sometimes a thoughtless runner will step off the base beforehand, allowing the first baseman to simply tag him out.

There are more sophisticated versions of the hidden ball trick. For example, the pitcher may step off and act like he's throwing the ball to first base. The first baseman then dives for the apparently erratic throw. He then jumps up and starts running after the ball (as do the right fielder and second baseman). If the runner buys into this charade,[3] he will take off for second base. The pitcher then throws the ball to the shortstop who makes the easy tag.

A DECEIVER OPPOSES THE CHURCH

I've always found it interesting that some Christians readily believe in angels but are quickly dismissive of demonic forces that oppose the church. And while I'm certainly not an authority on how much angelic merchandise is sold, about ten to twenty years ago, I noticed there was an obsession with angels in our culture. At the same time, people were dressing up in demonic costumes on Halloween, making light of the notion of a demonic reality.

Perhaps Hollywood has left so many warped images imprinted on our minds, that now we simply don't know what to believe. In the Christmas classic, *It's a Wonderful Life*, the angel (Clarence) appears as someone who is less than competent. He's an "angel second class" who is still trying to get his wings. In John Travolta's 1996 film *Michael*, the angel enjoys the pleasures of women and drinking. And the 1998 film *City of Angels* portrays an angel whose primary interest is love and the desire to become human.

Such fanciful images sometimes find their way into our psyche, and when they do, angelic forces are reduced to rather insignificant figures. In other words, if we think of heavenly angels as beings who lack power and holiness, then it's equally as easy to be indifferent to evil forces (fallen angels) we don't want to think about anyway. After all, people tend to believe in what makes them feel good, not bad.

The Bible is clear in that spiritual forces oppose God and his church. Leading the charge of these demonic forces is Satan. The New Testament references Satan in nineteen of the twenty-seven books (see Appendix A), and demons in thirteen (see Appendix B). Altogether, either Satan or his cohorts are mentioned in twenty of the twenty-seven books. The only exceptions are Galatians, Philippians, Titus, Philemon, 2 Peter, 2 John, and 3 John. And these are all short letters, with three of them being only one chapter in length.

Of specific interest, is that Satan is firmly described as a deceiver.[4] Revelation 12:9 says, "And the great dragon was thrown down, the serpent of old who is called the devil and Satan, who deceives the whole world." The emphasis is echoed in Revelation 20:2–3a, as it says, "And he laid hold of the dragon, the serpent of old, who is the devil and Satan, and bound him for a thousand years; and he threw him into the abyss, and shut it and sealed it over him, so that he would not deceive the nations any longer."

Genesis 3:13 is also clear in that the serpent (Satan) deceived Eve, a fact repeated by Paul in both 2 Corinthians 11:3 and

THE PICKOFF

1 Timothy 2:14. Our metaphor of the pickoff draws us specifically to Satan's ability to deceive.

NEW TESTAMENT WARNINGS OF DECEPTION

The New Testament is flooded with concerns of false teaching and deception. In fact, twenty-three of the twenty-seven books either explicitly or implicitly warn of deception (see Appendix C).

Jesus repeatedly told his followers to beware of false prophets. While some religious leaders are labeled as blind guides, others are described as ravenous wolves who appear in sheep's clothing.[5] The Apostle Paul warned the church of Satan's schemes and false teachers who taught strange doctrines. And the Apostle John often taught about the importance of truth, specifically as it relates to combating those who try to deceive us.

Truth is a prevalent theme in the New Testament, as Christ is "the way, the truth, and the life."[6] But Satan's mission is to distort the message of truth and deceive humankind. The New Testament frequently tells the church to be on her guard against deceptive teaching that pulls a person away from the truth of the gospel message. As an example, in the parable of the sower, Jesus told of how the devil comes and takes away the word from the heart of the hearer.[7] And yet, despite constant warnings of deception, believers often seem willing to view truth as something that is negotiable.

Having worked at a Bible college for over twenty years, I've seen some alumni shockingly lose their way. Recently, an alumna started a business where she advertises herself as an astrologist and psychic. She now claims she can communicate with angels. It's a heartbreaking reality that Christians, even some with a firm foundation of biblical truth, get picked off base.

Despite countless warnings to be on our guard against deception, we may wonder how some who once embraced the gospel eventually lose their way. The New Testament gives us several explanations, and here are a few.

Milk

Hebrews 5:12–6:1a says,

> For though by this time you ought to be teachers, you have need again for someone to teach you the elementary principles of the actual words of God, and you have come to need milk and not solid food. For everyone who partakes *only* of milk is unacquainted with the word of righteousness, for he is an infant. But solid food is for the mature, who because of practice have their senses trained to distinguish between good and evil. Therefore leaving the elementary teaching about the Christ, let us press on to maturity.

The lesson here is that we cannot be casual Christians who are not committed to the lordship of Christ. Making Christ one's Savior at a fixed point in time that is not followed by submission (obedience) is not an action that results in staying power. Pressing on toward maturity involves continual learning, accountability in the community of Christ, and a willingness to obey Christ in faith. In other words, things like Bible reading, church involvement, and prayer actually matter.

Itching Ears

Paul said the following to Timothy, "For *the* time will come when they will not tolerate sound doctrine; but *wanting* to have their ears tickled, they will accumulate for themselves teachers in accordance with their own desires, and they will turn their ears away from the truth and will turn aside to myths."[8]

We live in an age where people no longer concern themselves with objective truth; truth is simply whatever one wants it to be. This has become increasingly worse as political spin and conspiracy theories have caused some to become so entrenched in their personal beliefs that they no longer tolerate listening to others who may have differing points of view. Unfortunately, such thinking finds its way into the church too, as we pick and choose the biblical things we desire to "hear." This mindset even leads some to "adjust" the God of the Bible to a god that is more satisfying to their palate.

In a world that bombards us with messages like, "Do what makes you feel good," it's imperative that believers continually read the word of God and remain grounded in biblical truth. Furthermore, a steady connection with the body of Christ prevents us from being tossed around by every wind of doctrine and the deceitful scheming that comes from various sources.[9]

Running Aimlessly

In 1 Corinthians 9:24–26a, Paul encourages Christians to run the race with purpose—as to win. He says, "Do you not know that those who run in a race all run, but *only* one receives the prize? Run in such a way that you may win. Everyone who competes in the games exercises self-control in all things. So they *do it* to obtain a perishable wreath, but we an imperishable. Therefore, I run in such a way as not *to run* aimlessly."

And sadly, in Galatians 5:7, Paul also talks about Christians who were once running but eventually got detoured. He laments, saying, "You were running well; who hindered you from obeying the truth?" In these two passages, Paul ties running to both training and obedience. The Christian life involves an active life of "doing."[10]

Hebrews also has a familiar running reference and says, "Therefore, since we also have such a great cloud of witnesses surrounding us, let's rid ourselves of every obstacle and the sin which so easily entangles us, and let's run with endurance the race that is set before us."[11]

There are three important items of note from the Hebrews text. First, there are other believers in the race with us that we can look to for encouragement. If they can live by faith, then so can we. Second, we must make good decisions that will limit the temptation to be drawn into sin. And third, we must do the training necessary that enables us to run the long race before us.

THE ART OF DECEPTION

Lost Love

While these four items are certainly not an exhaustive list of reasons why people stop following Christ, it seems important to mention this final point. When Jesus spoke to the church at Ephesus (Rev 2:1–7), he commended them for their deeds, toil, perseverance, and lack of tolerance for evil people. And yet, despite these impressive traits, they had left their first love—Christ. It's a reminder to us that doing all the right things, while maintaining no relationship with our Lord, is a futile exercise we can only properly call "religion."

The Ephesian crisis informs us that biblical teaching must begin with Christ. Professing Christians who are never drawn into relationship with Christ cannot be called "Christ followers." Consequently, they are susceptible to false teaching as they do not know the voice of the Shepherd.[12]

DECEPTION IN THE CHURCH

The church is a light set on a hill that shines to all who are in darkness. And yet, in a fallen world, even the church is never perfect. For the record, I am pro-church. How can a Christian not be pro-church? Jesus is the head of the church, the Savior of the body, and loved the church so much that he gave his very life for her.[13]

But the church universal and the local church are not always the same. The church universal is the body of Christ, all believers who are Christ-followers. In other words, this is a massive group of people following after Jesus.

By contrast, the local church, while made of people, is often characterized as Such-and-Such Church—a specific group of people in a specific place. And being a specific church in a specific place, each local church takes on a unique identity. The problem is that the identity is sometimes less about Christ than something else.

The Pickoff

Let's take the seven churches in Revelation 2–3 as a case study of sorts. Here's a quick summary:

- 2:1–7 (Ephesus)—good deeds but lost their first love in Christ
- 2:8–11 (Smyrna)—persecuted and encouraged to remain faithful
- 2:12–17 (Pergamum)—false teaching
- 2:18–29 (Thyatira)—false teaching
- 3:1–6 (Sardis)—think they are alive, but are dead
- 3:7–13 (Philadelphia)—kept Jesus' word and have not denied his name
- 3:14–22 (Laodicea)—lukewarm

As five of the seven churches showed, where there are people, there are often problems. But as the churches at Smyrna and Philadelphia proved, it doesn't have to be that way. How do churches that start out well end up losing their first love, get wrapped up in false teaching, and/or become lukewarm in their faith? Like the people at Sardis, they think or profess one thing but live in a different reality. Ultimately, they are deceived and focus on the wrong things.

Unfortunately, our modern churches have also been accused of specializing in the wrong things. Here's a short list of some things you may have heard at some point:

- The Inwardly-focused Church—They are always working to build the local church but doing little (or nothing) to serve the community at large.

- The Attractional Church (In the past these were generally referred to as "seeker-sensitive" churches, and now they are often called "consumerist" or "market-driven.")—Visitors may see attractive stage designs, smoke machines, slick lighting, and well-produced videos. Topical self-help feel-good sermons (e.g., "5 Ways to Save Money and Prepare for Retirement") are often featured where preachers "proof-text"[14] for the purpose of the sermon at hand. But a common question is whether people are drawn by their own desires or to the lordship of Christ. And for those who are truly making Christ Savior, how deep will a shallow church take them in their faith?

- The Prosperity Church—Unfortunately, the health and wealth gospel is still alive and kicking.
- The Elitist Church—These "theologically superior" groups have an inability to work with others who do not agree with all of their beliefs. Unity is clearly not a priority.
- The Celebrity-driven Church—One must wonder if the preacher in these churches is more important to the members than Christ.
- The Traditions Church—Identification with the history of the church is great but holding to traditions that hinder the church from moving forward is a problem.

Besides some of these common problems seen in specific local churches, the church at large has allowed a host of deceptive lies to creep in and hinder the power of the gospel. Just consider the following:

- Overemphasis on attendance figures—Churches seem more concerned with large numbers than producing disciples of Christ. As Reggie McNeal said, we need to change the scorecard in the church.[15]
- Overemphasis on leadership—While the need for equipped leaders is a practical need, Jesus' message is clearly about serving, not leading. The leadership movement sends the wrong message and is implicitly self-serving. First and foremost, the church needs followers—followers of Christ.[16] The biblical message is to disciple people to become followers (servants of Christ). Not everyone should be striving to lead, as not everyone is called to do so. Furthermore, only those who zealously follow Christ have any business leading.

- Overemphasis on male leadership—To begin with, the entire question of who is in charge is the wrong question. Once again, the obsession with leadership clouds the truth of the gospel which focuses on serving. Both men and women are able to serve, and the Bible clearly recognizes prominent men and women who served in a variety of capacities.[17]
- Overemphasis on political leaders—When Christians put their trust in political leaders to change the world something is amiss. The only solution to true change is through a person's heart, and only Christ can change the heart. The church must look solely to Christ for true guidance.
- Overemphasis on God's love—Like a good parent who loves their child but also knows when to discipline them, God's love must stand in harmony with his other attributes (e.g., God is judge). This overemphasis has led to pluralism (i.e., various views about who God is) which distorts truth and ultimately leads to disregarding the authority of Scripture.

- Underemphasis on truth—Americans have a "me" and "what I want" mentality that has led to making truth subjective and submissive to self. With an obsession on large church attendance, boldly preaching truth from God's word is becoming more infrequent. After all, if we offend someone, they will leave the church and go elsewhere.
- Underemphasis on Scripture—While this certainly correlates to the previous point, the stress here is that preaching today often finds less of its basis in Scripture than it does elsewhere. Many topical sermons feature convenient translation hopping (to find a translation that says "what I want to say") which often leads to poor interpretation.
- Underemphasis on obedience—Again, with church attendance numbers being so important, church leaders dare not drive people away by challenging them to obey the Lord and his word. A church that doesn't stress obedience to the Lord

is bound to have morality problems and too many people who are authorities unto themselves.

- Underemphasis on relationship—We're living in an age of digital connectivity, and yet people are lonely and starving for real face-to-face relationships. Others desire discipleship, ministry care, and accountability. The church can provide the answer so many people are looking for, but she must put measures in place that ensure people actually get to know other believers on a personal level. Things like "small groups" must be emphasized and can't take a back seat to programs that do not promote togetherness.

THE BLURRING OF TRUTH

As we see from the churches in Revelation 2–3, and the problems of the current day, the church has to be on her guard against deceptive lies. In bombarding the church with deception, Satan behaves like a great pickoff artist who blurs the lines of what is legal/illegal or right/wrong. This blurring is what often leads to the previously mentioned problems of "overemphasis" and "underemphasis," as the issues often find their basis in something good. For example, sound leadership is vital so the church and its members can grow. But an overemphasis leads to a myriad of problems (e.g., looking to leaders instead of to Christ, looking to lead instead of to serve).

Satan often takes good things and twists them to his benefit. Just consider a few examples of how Satan skews the message from the Sermon on the Mount:[18]

- "You are the light of the world"[19]

    Jesus tells us we should not hide our lights, but Satan will tell us how irritated people get when we speak of God, and

The Pickoff

that can't be good for the Christian witness. Thus, Satan's influence has led to the popular notion that the best witness is a life well-lived. Of course, this is only a partial truth. Interestingly, in this passage Jesus' stress is neither to verbally proclaim the gospel message nor to live a holy life, but rather to display "good works" that others can see (i.e., let them shine).[20]

Because Jesus says the good works of Christians lead people to the Father,[21] Satan will stress other truths, twist the contextual meanings, and steer us away from Jesus' message. For example, in an attempt to derail our good intentions to help others, Satan will remind us that works do not save us (and he'll conveniently neglect the fact that works prove our faith is genuine[22]). Or he'll remind us of important church business that should be attended to. If there's nothing on the church agenda, Satan is always willing to turn our attention toward our family. We may recall, "if anyone does not provide for his own, and especially for those of his household, he has denied the faith and is worse than an unbeliever."[23] Before you know it, Jesus' words implicitly become thoughts such as, "You are a light (a blessing) in your church," or "You are the light of your family." And even if we wouldn't agree with those thoughts when expressed so blatantly, our actions may show that we've bought into them.

- "I say to you, love your enemies and pray for those who persecute you"[24]

Here, Jesus presents one of the most difficult challenges of all—loving even those we want nothing to do with. There's nothing wrong in admitting our hesitancy to love everyone. The problem is that Satan will jump on this admission and tell us that some are undeserving of love. The easy example, of course, is Adolf Hitler. After overseeing the Holocaust where approximately six million Jews were murdered, Satan boldly tells us that Hitler is an exception. Of course, so is Al Capone, the notorious mobster. And there's no doubt that after orchestrating the 9/11 attacks, neither Osama bin Laden nor any

THE ART OF DECEPTION

members of Al-Qaeda are deserving of love. Furthermore, as Satan may say, "The jerk that hit your car in the parking lot, never left a note, and then took off isn't deserving of love. And while we're at it, your boss treated you unfairly in that performance review, and she's not worthy of your love either."

The great strategy in this deceptive scheme is that exceptions simply lead to more exceptions. As Martin Luther King Jr. reminds us, however, "Jesus knew this was a hard teaching, sometimes so difficult that we will find it nearly impossible to follow. But Jesus 'wasn't playing.'"[25] "Loving others is exactly what God does, and he expects nothing less of his followers. In fact, our Lord loved those who nailed him to a cross."[26] And we must remember that we were once God's enemies.[27]

- "Ask, and it will be given to you; seek, and you will find; knock, and it will be opened to you"[28]

Because prayer brings us into direct communion with God, Satan will vigorously work to halt that effort. Distractions aside, Satan will work to convince us that prayer really isn't that necessary. I mean, "Isn't asking just proof of a lack of faith?" He may even play to our sinfulness and work to convince us that we are unworthy to receive "good gifts"[29] from the Father. "Oh, prayer won't hurt you, but it isn't that necessary either," says Satan. "Instead, why don't you just consult with one of your Christian friends. They'll have good advice for you."

Whether it's an atheistic argument (Why bother praying if there is no God?) or a good Christian truth (God already knows your situation), Satan is more than willing to try any deceptive tactic at his disposal. In fact, he is willing, able, and eager to find out if a believer will fall for one of them. After all, he would love to pick another runner off base.

The Pickoff

HOW TO RECOGNIZE DECEPTION

Satan may be a master pickoff artist, but like a great coach, God prepares his baserunners well. Our Lord not only tells us how to avoid being picked off, he also presents a clear plan for successful baserunning (e.g., making relationship with Christ the number one priority). One key to successful baserunning is to recognize deception so that we are not picked off.

In this world, deception has a voice. It can be heard via a sold-out convention center, a social media outlet, an addictive sitcom, a newspaper, or a neighbor. And being true to its name, deception also comes from unexpected sources, such as the pulpit or even the closest of friends and family. In the Sermon on the Mount, Jesus teaches us some valuable lessons about deception when he says,

> [15] Beware of the false prophets, who come to you in sheep's clothing, but inwardly are ravenous wolves. [16] You will know them by their fruits. Grapes are not gathered from thorn *bushes,* nor figs from thistles, are they? [17] So every good tree bears good fruit, but the bad tree bears bad fruit. [18] A good tree cannot bear bad fruit, nor can a bad tree bear good fruit. [19] Every tree that does not bear good fruit is cut down and thrown into the fire. [20] So then, you will know them by their fruits.
> [21] Not everyone who says to Me, 'Lord, Lord,' will enter the kingdom of heaven, but the one who does the will of My Father who is in heaven *will enter.* [22] Many will say to Me on that day, 'Lord, Lord, did we not prophesy in Your name, and in Your name cast out demons, and in Your name perform many miracles?' [23] And then I will declare to them, 'I never knew you; leave Me, you who practice lawlessness' (Matt 7:15–23).

In this eye-opening teaching, Jesus tells us that people aren't always who they appear to be. That's because false messengers of God often look like sheep (v. 15), sound like spokesmen for God (vv. 21–22), and even put on a good performance (v. 22). Despite the deception, Jesus says identification of such trickery is easy to spot—we must only inspect the fruit.

The Art of Deception

Problematic, however, is that Christians are overly hesitant to examine fruit. This results from our confusion in differentiating between "judging" and fruit inspection. Because judging others is so sinful, we rightly pay close attention to our Lord's warnings in Matthew 7:1–5. In fact, judging others is so bad, that regardless of our biblical knowledge on the topic, we are inherently aware.

But sometimes the enemy will remind us of the sin of judging others so we will look the other way when deceptive voices invade the body of Christ with false teaching. "You shouldn't judge the man of God. Look at the thousands who follow him. Surely, he is of God," says the enemy.

If we have concern for protecting Christian baserunners, it is our duty to look at the fruit. Jesus says, "Beware." There are deceptive voices among us. Sometimes they appear as ministers, politicians, or volunteers at church activities. They often say all the right things, boldly proclaiming Christ as Lord. It may even appear that God has used them to do great works for the kingdom. And yet, Jesus says to these fruitless pretenders, "I never knew you."

Unfortunately, Christians often appear to use a balancing scale to determine a leader's identity. For example, someone may say, "Yes, he did have multiple affairs, but he also helped so many people." This type of evaluation is possibly the result of a fear of judging, but it's also a bizarre approach that completely ignores Jesus' warnings to us. He says, "You will know them by their fruits."

When the Christian comes to understand the imperative of fruit inspection, the enemy may help us recall that Christians should also be forgiving. And while this is certainly true (because we rightly recognize God as the Judge), it in no way means that we should allow those with bad fruit to lead the church. This is precisely why Paul provides qualifications for leaders.[30]

Recalling the imperative of fruit inspection will also help us see through a favorite tactic of Satan, as he will even remind us of the power of grace. He'll say, "God's grace is great. Just have faith in God and live in any manner you wish." Of course, the Apostle Paul calls such talk absurd,[31] but Satan will work to steer us away from that truth. This is such a common tactic of Satan, that Jude

4 explicitly warns us of ungodly people who creep into the church "who turn the grace of our God into indecent behavior and deny our only Master and Lord, Jesus Christ."

Satan has many deceptive weapons in his arsenal. Yet, to see through his deception we must be diligent in fruit inspection. Of course, to recognize fruits that are of God, we must be well-acquainted with God's word. Thus, the enemy will do everything in his power to keep us from hearing what God has said to us.

"You don't need to read the Bible," he says, "You can hear the word at church." If believed, this lie can be devastating to the believer. In following this advice of laziness, we put our sole trust in the preacher instead of God. The enemy also floods society with ideas that attempt to chop the power of God's word off at its knees, telling people that the Bible is just an ancient book of myths with outdated beliefs. He might even tell us that Jesus was a good person, but he surely wasn't the Savior of the world.

A popular lie the enemy successfully floats is that we may essentially pick and choose what to believe or not believe in the Bible. He'll say something like, "Mental illness is real, but you need not be concerned about demonic influence. That's just what people believed before they became enlightened." This is a classic satanic half-truth, as both mental illness and demonic influence are realities.

In drawing us away from the truth in God's word, the enemy ultimately attempts to draw us away from The Word—Jesus. Jesus is the truth, the truth that enables us to see through the deceptive lies of the enemy. We must remain steady in relationship with him and in the pages of his word.

THE WRAP-UP

In her fictional novel *The Sacred Band*, author Janet Morris says, "Deception is a tactic: use it. Do whatever it takes to win." Surely, this echoes the sentiment of a great pickoff artist. Yet, despite the attempts of the enemy, our Lord exposes this ploy, even telling us how to recognize and avoid it. Like the churches at Smyrna and Philadelphia who received commendation from Jesus (Rev 2–3), we can prevent baserunning blunders and remain faithful and keep Jesus' commands.

CHAPTER 2

Quick Feet

WHEREAS LEFT-HANDED PITCHERS WITH great pickoff moves to first base master the art of deception, right-handed pitchers are at a great disadvantage. Most often, they settle for simply trying to keep the runner close to the bag. There are, however, some righties with a specific skill set that promotes pickoff success, like quick feet that enable them to spin and throw to first with astonishing speed.

James Shields[32] is a pitcher who comes to mind. In 2011, he recorded thirteen pickoffs and was the first right-handed pitcher to lead the majors since Charlie Hough recorded sixteen in 1988. Some pitchers, like Shields, win the battle because they have quicker feet than the runner who tries to retreat to the base. Having quick feet is a great tool for right-handers trying to keep runners close.

Shields was so shifty that he even studied "the layout of each infield."[33] At each park, he would "measure the distance from first base to the outer edge of the dirt cutout.[34] That way, when he peeks at the runner, Shields can accurately measure his lead based on how close he is to the cutout."[35] Shields was quick and informed. When runners duel with a pitcher like that, they must stay on their toes and be ready to quickly respond. When they don't, they pay the price.

Quick Feet
UNDERESTIMATING THE ENEMY

When a pitcher like Shields is on the mound, runners ought to be cautious. Unfortunately, some take the task at hand (remaining on base) far too lightly. And once again, this is a perfect metaphor to consider as we contemplate Satan's effectiveness at picking Christians off the narrow road.

Avid baseball fans will readily admit how frustrating it is to witness a baserunner get picked off first base by a right-handed pitcher. Sometimes, it even seems a bit mind-boggling. While an ideal lead for the runner is about 9–12 feet,[36] allowances must be made for a great pickoff artist. While the pitcher is approximately 63–64 feet from first base, a guy with quick feet can snap a throw over there swiftly. Thus, a smart baserunner must shorten up his lead to ensure safety on the bases when facing a pitcher with an accomplished pickoff history. Yet, because runners still get picked off, we must ask why this happens.

Inaccurate Assessment

Runners need to know the pitcher they are dealing with, but sometimes they fail to properly assess the pitcher's abilities. Furthermore, they occasionally fail to properly assess their own abilities. This serves to remind us that baserunners need to be at their very best and remain properly prepared for running the Christian race.

It must be pointed out that baseball players can clearly see their opponent standing on the mound, but even then, they sometimes fail to take the threat seriously. When it concerned throwing over to first base, Chicago Cubs southpaw Jon Lester was rather infamous for having the yips.[37] It had gotten so bad, that at some point, he simply stopped trying to throw over. Knowing this, St. Louis Cardinals outfielder Tommy Pham tried to take full advantage of the situation (June 3, 2017). So, Pham walked approximately twenty feet off the base and planned to take off for second, when suddenly Lester picked off his first runner in two years. When

The Pickoff

Pham was asked if he thought Lester would throw over, he simply said, "Nope. You just go off what he's done in the past."[38]

If a baseball player can so easily dismiss a visible threat, consider how much easier it is for the Christian to make this mistake when they're contending with an invisible enemy. It's no wonder the enemy is often dismissed as a non-threat to their success. But overlooking this danger can be disastrous, as God's word presents enemy forces as real entities bent on destroying humanity. Thus, it's appropriate to conclude that one of the first things the Christian can do in preparation for victory is to acknowledge the potential threat of an enemy bent on picking off Christian baserunners.

The Apostle Paul tells us that the god of this world blinds the minds of unbelievers.[39] While Paul places this within the context of prevention from seeing the light of the gospel, it's a valid question to wonder how Satan attempts to blind all of us from particular realities—one being his very existence.

For a moment, imagine the absurdity of a baserunner who is oblivious to the pitcher on the mound desiring to pick him off base. This is the very thing the enemy of God attempts to accomplish with God's people. Satan works to cloud our judgment, so we will completely dismiss him as a real threat. He tells us, "Demonic forces are not real. They are just fanciful characters that spur the imagination and strike fear into children. There may be a god, but there are not evil forces working against humanity. The whole idea is like believing in Greek mythology."

Yet, Paul exclaimed that the church should not be ignorant of Satan's schemes.[40] As Christian baserunners, we must face the unpleasant fact that a powerful entity wishes to pick us off base. Thus, it's imperative that we are prepared.

The apostle takes up this theme again in Ephesians 6 when he encourages us to "take up the full armor of God."[41] Note the reason Paul provides in verses 10–12 before launching into this well-known section. He says,

> [10] Finally, be strong in the Lord and in the strength of His might. [11] Put on the full armor of God, so that you will be able to stand firm against the schemes of the devil. [12] For

our struggle is not against flesh and blood, but against the rulers, against the powers, against the world forces of this darkness, against the spiritual *forces* of wickedness in the heavenly *places.*

If we are to avoid being picked off base, we must first know what we are up against. In essence, it's this very knowledge that provides the impetus for putting on the armor of God. Just stop and think about that. If there were no real enemy, Paul would never have provided this section on the armor of God.

It's also critical that we put on the "full" (or "whole") armor of God, as the apostle says we must do everything we can to stand firm.[42] He continues in Ephesians 6 by saying,

> [14] Stand firm therefore, having belted your waist with truth, and having put on the breastplate of righteousness, [15] and having strapped on your feet the preparation of the gospel of peace; [16] in addition to all, taking up the shield of faith with which you will be able to extinguish all the flaming arrows of the evil *one.* [17] And take the helmet of salvation and the sword of the Spirit, which is the word of God.

Putting on the armor is what Paul would call appropriate preparation. It's so important that books have been devoted to this single topic. Appropriate attire (belt, helmet, etc.) helps ensure victory. Neglect of even one of these items leaves a chink in one's armor. And such neglect can leave the Christian vulnerable to the enemy's attacks.

Paul understood the necessity of accurate assessment. First, there is an enemy scheming against us. Second, we are vulnerable to the enemy's scheming. But third, our Lord has given us all we need to stand against the enemy. We must know his truth and surrender our very lives to the truth of Jesus our Lord. In Christ, the fully committed Christian can always withstand the assault of the enemy.

As we return to our baseball metaphor, one thing must be clearly understood—occasionally the pitcher is simply better than the runner. But this is only the case when the runner attempts to invent their own rules for living the Christian life. Christians who ignore God's clear directions and dare to challenge the pitcher on their own terms are always headed toward the dugout, head down, in utter embarrassment.

Flirtation

Right-handed, quick-footed pitchers like Shields also find pickoff success because sometimes the runners want to push the limits in seeing how far they can get off the base. In other words, they become victims of flirtation. While this can also be an example of incorrect assessment, it remains distinct in that sometimes it's simply one's faulty state of mind that encourages the runner to take one step too many.

> *Christians who flirt with danger are headed for trouble.*

Likewise, Christians who flirt with danger are headed for trouble. Paul reminds us that "the wages of sin is death."[43] While Christ-followers are no longer slaves to sin, we are not to flirt with it. In building to this grand statement, the apostle tells us that sin should not reign in our bodies and that we should not allow our bodies to be used as "instruments of unrighteousness." In Christ, we are now "slaves for obedience"/"slaves to righteousness."

Yet, Satan entices us by telling us how harmless a little flirtation is. In fact, sometimes he says, "A little flirtation feels good, and it won't really hurt anyone. You can control yourself and pull out of this situation when it begins to get messy."

Christians who maintain a casual attitude toward sin neither understand the power of sin, nor the power of Christ that set us free from it. Sin is a powerful master that drives us away from God. Unfortunately, Samson may provide the best example of how continual flirtation with sin can have disastrous results.

Samson's story[44] is a remarkable one. Samson was the son of Manoah. While we're not given the name of Manoah's wife, we're told that she was infertile. But an angel of the Lord appeared to her and revealed that she would have a son. The angel said, "And now, be careful not to drink wine or strong drink, nor eat any unclean thing. For behold, you will conceive and give birth to a son, and no razor shall come upon his head, for the boy shall be a Nazirite to God from the womb; and he will begin to save Israel from the hands of the Philistines." Judges 13:24 says, "So the woman gave birth to a son, and named him Samson; and the child grew up and the Lord blessed him."

Samson became of man of great strength and judged Israel for twenty years. But Judges 16 begins by providing a sign to his eventual downfall, as verse 1 says, "Now Samson went to Gaza and saw a prostitute there, and had relations with her." Shortly afterward, he falls in love with Delilah, who was most likely a Philistine. As soon as the Philistine governors get wind of this relationship, they essentially ask her to serve as a double agent for their benefit. They said, "Entice him, and see where his great strength *lies* and how we can overpower him so that we may bind him to humble him. Then we will each give you 1,100 *pieces* of silver."

Delilah is not immediately successful, as we read of three occasions where Samson simply "toys"[45] with her. But verse 16 says that "she pressed him daily with her words and urged him, that his soul was annoyed to death."

So, here's what we have. A man set aside to do God's work puts himself in a threatening situation by flirting with danger. Each of the three toying episodes concludes with Delilah saying, "The Philistines are upon you, Samson." Thus, there is no mistaking Samson as a fool who just thinks the woman he loves wants to know his innermost secrets. Ultimately, she pulls out the "if you love me" card in Judges 16:15. Samson knew he was flirting with trouble—and eventually trouble is exactly what he got!

Judges 16:17 says, "So he told her all *that was in* his heart and said to her, 'A razor has never come on my head, for I have been a Nazirite to God from my mother's womb. If I am shaved, then my strength will leave me and I will become weak and be like any *other* man.'" After the confession, Delilah wastes no time informing the Philistine leaders that they now have their man.

The Pickoff

After luring Samson to sleep, Delilah has his hair cut off, and the Spirit of God departs from Samson. The sad story continues with Samson having his eyes gouged out, being shackled with bronze chains, being sentenced to the slave labor task of grinding grain at the prison, and finally, becoming a circus act for onlookers wanting cheap entertainment.

While Samson's hair grows back (a sign that the Lord will have the last say in this story), and he destroys the temple of Dagon and the three thousand Philistines celebrating sacrifices to their pagan god, this story cannot be construed as a master plan of God. In truth, it's the depressing story of a servant of God who took one too many steps off first base.

THE CHRISTIAN IN RESPONSE

The quick feet of a great right-handed pickoff artist bring another thought to mind—when the enemy attacks, the Christian must respond quickly. To illustrate, let's return to the Sermon on the Mount.

Matthew 5:21–48 contains what scholars often call the "six antitheses." I like to refer to them as six deeper truths. With each item, Jesus says something like, "You have heard it was said . . . but I say." Here, Jesus discusses the following: murder (21–26), adultery (27–30), divorce (31–32), vows (33–37), revenge (38–42), and hate (43–47).

One of the thought-provoking aspects of this passage is how Jesus takes the first item (murder, 21–26) and describes how previous sinful actions can accelerate into something worse. Jesus moves from the topics of anger and judgmental attitudes concerning the worthlessness of someone else into murder itself. He implicitly says that uncontrolled anger can lead to something such as homicide. In other words, festering unhealthy thoughts about a person's worthlessness can lead to the action of eliminating them altogether.

With the second item (adultery, 27–30), Jesus talks about how lusting after another person leads to adultery of the heart, which in turn can lead to the physical act itself. Both sins (murder and adultery) can be avoided by quick response to the initial thoughts.

When unholy thoughts enter the mind (sometimes influenced by the enemy himself), we must quickly respond with appropriate Christlike action. For example, in discussing how lust leads to adultery, Jesus uses overstatement to help us understand the imperative of taking quick action. He says, "Now if your right eye is causing you to sin, tear it out and throw it away from you; for it is better for you to lose one of the parts of your *body*, than for your whole body to be thrown into hell."[46]

Something like adultery doesn't just happen. Thus, when roaming eyes and lustful thoughts take place, we should take immediate corrective action. In baseball terms, when the pitcher makes any type of move toward first, we must immediately retreat to the bag—there is never time for hesitation. Similarly, when a Christian is tempted by sin, the temptation must always be met with quick preventive measures.

THE WRAP-UP

New York Yankees great Yogi Berra was a member of ten World Series championship teams, the only player to accomplish such an incredible feat. And yet, the Hall of Famer is probably best known today for his humorous sayings, called "Yogi-isms." One of his quotes applies here, as he once said, "The other teams could make trouble for us if they win."

Yes, opponents can make trouble for us. We should never, never, never underestimate the enemy. Thus, we must properly assess our opponent, and knowing the opponent is a threat, we should not flirt with disaster.

We need to come to the realization that when unprotected by the full armor of God, our abilities to withstand the temptations of sin are futile. Thus, to avoid being picked off, when we perceive a threat to living a life that honors God, we must quickly retreat into the safety of God's arms. Living in obedience to God ensures a lifetime of successful baserunning.

CHAPTER 3

Caught Sleeping

PITCHERS TYPICALLY COME TO mind when we think of pickoff artists, but we must not forget the catchers who love to get in on the action. One such great pickoff artist was Hall of Famer Johnny Bench. Widely regarded as the greatest catcher to ever play the game, Bench excelled both offensively and defensively.

A snapshot of his dominance was displayed during the 1976 World Series. His Cincinnati Reds swept the New York Yankees in four games, with Bench winning the MVP along the way. He hit .533 with 2 HR and 6 RBI, collecting two hits in each of the four games. Bench also cut down one of the two runners who tried to steal and even picked a runner off second base.[47] Bench finished his career with sixty-two pickoffs.[48]

A runner should never get picked off by the catcher. Thus, when it happens, you'll often hear the announcer say that the runner was caught sleeping. This metaphor helps explain how the catcher was able to catch the runner by surprise. Of course, pitchers sometimes find runners sleeping too, but the phrase is most often associated with the astute catcher who observes an inattentive baserunner.

When a runner temporarily "zones out" and fails to concentrate on the task at hand, they become susceptible to being picked off base. Unlike being deceived or simply getting beat by a pitcher with quick feet, getting caught sleeping will drive the manager crazy. There's an old adage in sports that goes something like this: "Physical mistakes happen, but there's no excuse for mental mistakes." Getting caught sleeping is a rally killer, and it has a way of shifting momentum.

THE IMPERATIVE OF REMAINING AWAKE AND ALERT

New Testament writers share the concern of getting caught sleeping, as they often encourage Christ-followers to remain "awake" or "alert." The Greek word[49] most often used to communicate this is *grēgoreō*, which literally means to "keep awake." Figuratively, it means to "be on the alert, be watchful (cf. keep one's eyes open)." A similar word,[50] though only used sparingly, is *agrypneō*.[51] It literally means to "keep oneself awake, be awake" and metaphorically means to "keep watch over something, guard, care for it."

Jesus especially, in addition to New Testament writers, uses these words in relation to the Second Coming. But they also use the words to speak of how Christians must be aware of the potential danger surrounding them so they may remain safe. Six passages are of particular interest.[52] Most interesting is that five of the six passages are among parting words. In fact, even the last one in 1 Thessalonians 5 leads into the final words of the letter.

Final words are important. We may think of a nervous parent giving final instructions to their child before their first day of school. In keeping with our sports theme, we may be reminded of a coach giving a final word of instruction as a timeout ends. We often view final words as the very most important thing being said. In fact, we've all heard someone say something like, "If you forget everything I said, please just remember this one last thing."

Also, final words often come from the heart. This is why Paul often sends greetings to his friends in the concluding words of his letters. It's also why we often hug and say, "I love you" as we leave someone's home on a holiday. Words are important, and final words are like an exclamation point.

The Pickoff

Peter provides one of the texts that are of interest. As he concludes his first letter, he says the following: "Be of sober *spirit*, be on the alert. Your adversary, the devil, prowls around like a roaring lion, seeking someone to devour."[53] He continues by saying, "So resist him, firm in *your* faith." In essence, Peter's message is, "Don't get caught sleeping. The enemy is a real threat. So, we must always be alert."

Paul provides us with the other five passages. His words to the Corinthians sound somewhat similar to Peter's words. In 1 Corinthians 16:13 Paul said, "Be on the alert, stand firm in the faith, act like men, be strong." Because the words Paul uses in verse 13 are not tied to the people his addressing (Timothy, vv. 10–11; Apollos, v. 12; Stephanas and Achaicus, vv. 15–18; Aquila and Prisca, v. 19), they almost seem a bit out of place. But as one reads chapter 16 in its entirety, it becomes clear that these words are given within the context of successful ministry. They stand out as critical words of final instruction that Paul leaves with the brothers and sisters at Corinth.

Acts 20 provides another important reference, as Paul gives some final words to the elders at Ephesus. He says,

> [28] Be on guard for yourselves and for all the flock, among which the Holy Spirit has made you overseers, to shepherd the church of God which He purchased with His own blood. [29] I know that after my departure savage wolves will come in among you, not sparing the flock; [30] and from among your own selves men will arise, speaking perverse things to draw away the disciples after them. [31] Therefore, be on the alert, remembering that night and day for a period of three years I did not cease to admonish each one with tears.[54]

This message is notable, as Paul anticipates this is the last time he will ever see them.[55] He even makes mention of the three years he spent in Ephesus. Thus, we may see these words as coming from a deep place of love for them. So, what does he say? First, "Be on your guard." And second, "Be on the alert." Paul knows that the enemy would love to take his three years of effort and destroy them by sending in false teachers who will pick off Christian baserunners. Thus, Paul does all he can do. He gives them the final critical words they need to hear and then prays with them.⁵⁶

Paul's final instructions to the Colossians began with the words, "Devote yourselves to prayer, keeping alert in it with *an attitude of* thanksgiving."⁵⁷ Ephesians 6:18 also involves prayer, and immediately follows Paul's description of the armor of God. Paul says, "With every prayer and request, pray at all times in the Spirit, and with this in view, be alert with all perseverance and *every* request for all the saints."

In both passages, Paul reminds us that prayer is an important ingredient in successful baserunning. We must be alert in it because neglect of prayer is hazardous to the church. First, in the Colossians passage Paul connects prayer to thanksgiving, reminding us that mindful prayer is thankful prayer. Second, Paul continues in both passages by asking the saints to pray for his ability to effectively share the gospel.⁵⁸ This is critical as new runners must always be added to the basepaths. And third, to the Ephesians, Paul linked alertness with perseverance (continual prayer), as well praying in the Spirit. In other words, alert baserunners pray in cooperation with the Holy Spirit. It's this type of alertness that has continual concern for the welfare of fellow baserunners. From these two passages we may conclude that alert baserunning is continually mindful of the good things of God, always looks to add new baserunners, and aids in the prevention of teammates being picked off base.

The final passage to note is 1 Thessalonians 5:1–11 which says,

> ¹ Now as to the periods and times, brothers *and sisters*, you have no need *of anything* to be written to you. ² For you yourselves know full well that the day of the Lord is coming just like a thief in the night. ³ While they are saying, "Peace and safety!" then sudden destruction will

The Pickoff

come upon them like labor pains upon a pregnant woman, and they will not escape. **4** But you, brothers *and sisters*, are not in darkness, so that the day would overtake you like a thief; **5** for you are all sons of light and sons of day. We are not of night nor of darkness; **6** so then, let's not sleep as others do, but let's be alert and sober.
7 For those who sleep, sleep at night, and those who are drunk, get drunk at night. **8** But since we are of *the* day, let's be sober, having put on the breastplate of faith and love, and as a helmet, the hope of salvation. **9** For God has not destined us for wrath, but for obtaining salvation through our Lord Jesus Christ, **10** who died for us, so that whether we are awake or asleep, we will live together with Him. **11** Therefore, encourage one another and build one another up, just as you also are doing.

While the passage's primary topic is the day of the Lord, it leads into the concluding words of the letter. Like many other New Testament usages of the word "alert" (*grēgoreō*), in verse 6 Paul uses the word to speak of those in the light who should not be caught off guard by future events. However, Paul usage of this word here extends beyond merely being alert, as once again he uses the term in conjunction with the armor of God.

In Ephesians 6, Paul describes the armor of God as consisting of a belt, a breastplate, footwear, a shield, a helmet, and a sword. He immediately followed the armor by talking about having alertness in prayer. The imagery of 1 Thessalonians 5:8 is a noticeable connection, as Paul talks about putting on a breastplate and helmet. But in this case, Paul precedes the armor by talking about being alert and sober.

"Sober" is contrasted with "drunk,"[59] and in a figurative sense, to be sober means to "be free from every form of mental and spiritual drunkenness," as well as free from confusion.[60] In essence, the apostle uses the words "alert" and "sober" in tandem as he stresses clear-mindedness as critical to putting on the armor which ensures protection (i.e., salvation vs. wrath, v. 9). In fact, Paul likens the helmet to salvation,[61] a clear image of safety.

As previously mentioned, Paul employs the armor of God in Ephesians 6 as a means "to stand firm against the schemes of the devil." While in 1 Thessalonians 5 Paul does not mention the enemy, alertness and armor are used to address safety on the base-paths—the same message provided in Ephesians 6.

In summary, for our context, the six passages that stress being alert can be understood as follows:

- 1 Corinthians 16:13 speaks to successful ministry—what we may call successful baserunning.

- Colossians 4:2 and Ephesians 6:18 speak to the importance of prayer—a key to adding new baserunners and preventing teammates from being picked off base.

- 1 Peter 5:8, Acts 20:31, and 1 Thessalonians 5:6 respectively speak about the devil, false teachers, and salvation—each connecting alertness to safety.

We're charged to remain alert, as it's a clear requirement for successful baserunning. Of course, as was shown in previous chapters, the enemy will work to make us dismiss this need for alertness as nonsense. He will say, "The threats of most importance are the real things that threaten mankind, things like global warming and nuclear annihilation." And while these may be true concerns, they are not the focus of God's command to be alert. God wants us to be wake up to the fact that our primary struggle is against the enemy of our souls.

DISTRACTED BY THE WRONG ISSUES

In 2018, Minnesota Twins catcher Willians Astudillo used a little trickery to pick a runner off who completely zoned out.[62] What made this pickoff particularly humiliating for New York Yankees outfielder Shane Robinson, is that he was pinch running. After the pitch was made, Astudillo casually kept looking straight at the pitcher and then nonchalantly made a "no-look" throw to first base. In doing so, he caught Robinson walking back to the

The Pickoff

bag while looking at the pitcher, as he wasn't focused on the first baseman who now had the ball. It was so bad that one of the announcers simply commented by saying, "Caught napping, that's embarrassing."

For some unknown reason, Robinson was distracted by the pitcher. Likewise, Christians can get distracted by the wrong issues. While baserunners know they should remain focused on knowing where the ball is at all times, we may rightly ask which things should remain the focus for Christian baserunners. As we remain consistent with the baseball metaphor, we should remember that the ultimate goal of the baserunner is to score, and the same is true in the Christian life. Thus, the most important thing that Christian baserunners should be focused on is maintaining a relationship with Christ, as Jesus is the way[63] and the door.[64]

While always working on a relationship with Christ seems so obvious, the enemy may try to convince us that this is self-serving. He may say, "You don't need to pray or read your Bible right now. You need to serve others. Go mow your elderly neighbor's lawn. You know he/she needs help." In this way, the enemy works to distract us by doing good works that ultimately drive us away from the Savior. While it's true that Christians can't live in seclusion from the world, we must maintain a healthy harmony between personal growth and service to others. Furthermore, the lawn can be mowed after our time with Christ. In fact, the conversation with the neighbor is bound to be more fruitful when consistent communion with Christ is taking place.

In baseball, it's also common to hear someone in the dugout say, "Keep the line moving." In other words, the team is always looking for more baserunners, as baserunners represent potential runs. Again, this is also a priority for Christians, as Jesus gave us the Great Commission in Matthew 28:19–20. It says, 19 "Go, therefore, and make disciples of all the nations, baptizing them in the name of the Father and the Son and the Holy Spirit, 20 teaching them to follow all that I commanded you; and behold, I am with you always, to the end of the age." These final words in Matthew's gospel account underline the importance of the Christian mission.

CAUGHT SLEEPING

As the book of Acts opens[65] with the resurrected Jesus appearing to the disciples over a forty-day period, Jesus leaves a few final words before ascending into heaven. He said, "You will receive power when the Holy Spirit has come upon you; and you shall be My witnesses both in Jerusalem and in all Judea, and Samaria, and as far as the remotest part of the earth." It's clear that sharing the gospel throughout the world is a priority.

While we may note many important components that make up living the Christian life, two items of great importance stand out as critical.

- First, maintaining a relationship with Christ is imperative, as relationship leads to growth and perseverance.
- Second, we must share the good news of Christ with all of humanity, making disciples for Christ.

Hereafter, these will be referred to as critical elements one and two. These are clear and simple priorities from which we must not be distracted. Of course, they remind us of our baseball game.

- First, take care of yourself on the basepaths.
- Second, encourage others to join in on the scoring, and coach others so they may run the bases successfully.

As we consider these basics, we should also reflect on Jesus' prayer for us in John 17. While the church traditionally called Matthew 6:9–13 "The Lord's Prayer," it has been renamed "The Model Prayer," as Jesus doesn't pray but explains how we should pray. John 17:1–26, however, may properly be named "The Lord's Prayer" because it's here where we see the lengthiest prayer of Jesus.

Think about it, Jesus prayed for us! There can be no doubt that this prayer demands our full attention, as he knows exactly what we need. While the entire chapter provides Jesus' prayer, his prayer for us really picks up in John 17:9 with the following,

> ⁹ I ask on their behalf; I do not ask on behalf of the world, but on the behalf of those whom You have given Me, because they are Yours; ¹⁰ and all things that are Mine are

Yours, and Yours are Mine; and I have been glorified in them. **11** I am no longer *going to be* in the world; and *yet* they themselves are in the world, and I am coming to You. Holy Father, keep them in Your name, *the name* which You have given Me, so that they may be one just as We *are*. **12** While I was with them, I was keeping them in Your name, which You have given Me; and I guarded them, and not one of them perished except the son of destruction, so that the Scripture would be fulfilled.

13 But now I am coming to You; and these things I speak in the world so that they may have My joy made full in themselves. **14** I have given them Your word; and the world has hated them because they are not of the world, just as I am not of the world. **15** I am not asking You to take them out of the world, but to keep them away from the evil one. **16** They are not of the world, just as I am not of the world. **17** Sanctify them in the truth; Your word is truth. **18** Just as You sent Me into the world, I also sent them into the world. **19** And for their sakes I sanctify Myself, so that they themselves also may be sanctified in truth.

20 I am not asking on behalf of these alone, but also for those who believe in Me through their word, **21** that they may all be one; just as You, Father, *are* in Me and I in You, that they also may be in Us, so that the world may believe that You sent Me.

22 The glory which You have given Me I also have given to them, so that they may be one, just as We are one; **23** I in them and You in Me, that they may be perfected in unity, so that the world may know that You sent Me, and You loved them, just as You loved Me. **24** Father, I desire that they also, whom You have given Me, be with Me where I am, so that they may see My glory which You have given Me, for You loved Me before the foundation of the world.

25 Righteous Father, although the world has not known You, yet I have known You; and these have known that You sent Me; **26** and I have made Your name known to them, and will make it known, so that the love with which You loved Me may be in them, and I in them.

There are four key takeaways we must note, as they reinforce the two critical elements of maintaining relationship with Christ and sharing the gospel. First, Jesus prays for our safety and perseverance. This is a feature that is repeated[66] throughout the prayer, being expressed in three distinct ways. It is shown in verse 15 when Jesus says, "to keep them away from the evil one." The master pickoff artist is always looking to catch runners off guard, and Jesus reminds us that Judas became one of his victims.[67]

Jesus' concern for perseverance is also seen in verses 11–12 and 24 in the phrases, "keep them in Your name," "I was keeping them," "I guarded them," and "be with Me where I am." In these statements, Jesus shows deep concern for our persistence in following him. Also, Jesus speaks of us being in fellowship with him (v. 21, "that they also may be in Us" and v. 23, "I in them"). These two statements not only speak to perseverance, but directly to Jesus' concern that we be in relationship with him for eternity. Each of these items reinforce the critical element that we must continue in relationship with Christ, which leads to growth and perseverance.

A second key found in John 17 is Jesus' prayer for unity. Like the theme of perseverance, Jesus' concern for unity is also seen throughout.[68] Not only is the phrase "may be one" used three times, but Jesus prays that we would be "perfected in unity." The unity Jesus prays for is a comprehensive one, as he prays for Christians to have unity with one another, just as the Father and Son enjoy unity, and just as Jesus and his followers have unity.

In both verses 21 and 23, Jesus prays for unity "so that the world may believe" that the Father sent him. Clearly, unity among the followers of Christ is key to others believing the gospel message. This reinforces critical element two—that we are to share the good news of Christ.

Furthermore, Jesus leads into his prayer for unity by saying, "I am not asking on behalf of these alone, but also for those who believe in Me through their word" (v. 20). Note the latter half of verse 20, as Jesus is praying for all future believers who had not yet accepted the gospel. This group of future disciples also reinforces

The Pickoff

that we must make disciples for Christ. Here we learn that good discipling involves teaching the value of unity.

A third item of note in John 17 is that Jesus twice prays for the Father to "sanctify" his followers "in truth."[69] Knowing the truth enables one to stand against the onslaught of false teaching, helping us to persevere in the faith. Truth begins with Christ, as Jesus is "the truth."[70] Through relationship with the truth, and adherence to the truth, we can endure in the faith (each of these speak to the critical element of our relationship with Christ). And, of course, teaching the truth is also part of the second critical element, as we must proclaim the truth to unbelievers and believers alike.

Since we're dealing with a pickoff artist, we should note that the enemy would love to have us so hyper-focused on one issue that we neglect another. For example, a church may sacrifice truth for the sake of unity. We may think of a church that is so bent on maintaining unity among its members that they fail to report abuse in the church. Likewise, in a quest to assert truth, unity is sometimes sacrificed. An example may be one church who can't work with another because they are overly concerned with contamination of their doctrinal positions.

These are the tactics of a deceptive pitcher who would love to catch us sleeping. As Shane Robinson was caught staring at the pitcher when he should have been looking at the catcher, we can also get distracted by the wrong things. Jesus prays for us to live in the harmony of maintaining both unity and truth.

While the first three items from Jesus' prayer in John 17 were provided with great repetitive emphasis, this fourth, and final item is altogether different. In fact, Jesus actually mentions two things that have been combined into one larger thought. He prays that we would have his "joy,"[71] as well as the "love" of the Father.[72] The common denominator is that both should be characteristic of the believer, as representatives of God should be joyful people who love others. And, of course, joy is often the result of love. These are both key principles that address both critical issues as they are the results of maintaining a relationship with Christ and they are part of sound disciple-making.

In summary, in Jesus' prayer, four concerns are mentioned: (1) our safety, perseverance, and eternal relationship with him; (2) our unity which leads to effective Christian witness, and is an important trait for disciples of Christ; (3) that we live in the truth; (4) and that we have both the joy and love of God. We can see that Jesus' prayer for us reinforces the two critical elements Christians must be focused on as they live the Christian life: maintaining relationship with Christ and sharing the gospel/making disciples.

It's essential to remember that distracted baserunners are vulnerable, and that we sometimes get distracted with issues (even good issues) which move us away from our highest priorities. Therefore, we must always keep our eyes fixed on Jesus,[73] as Christ is the North Star[74] to which we must always orient our movements.

While it's tempting to detail so many things that may distract us (e.g., traditions, politics, offerings, attendance figures, social issues, church programs), in baseball, coaches don't dwell as much on what you shouldn't be doing—they emphasize what you must be doing. For example, when a right-handed pitcher has engaged the pitching rubber, runners are often taught to watch his right foot because the pitcher cannot spin and throw toward first base without lifting his heel. Because this is not the only indication of where a pitcher is throwing, some coaches teach runners to look at the left heel, front shoulder, or back knee. Regardless, the point here is that runners are taught to remain attentive to the critical issue at hand.

Of course, the metaphor is not perfect. Christ will often have us involved in many good things, such as social issues or church programs. But we must not miss the fact that we cannot be overly consumed in any single thing that distracts us from our highest priorities. As an example, many of us have seen the Sunday School teacher of thirty years who never attends class herself. Such habits may raise the question whether this person takes personal discipleship seriously.

The Pickoff

We may also think of a church leader who promotes church programs the people love but fails to instill a sense of evangelistic concern in reaching the community for Jesus. Effective church leaders (and coaches) don't just do things to make everyone happy, they work at what must be done for the sake of success. Thus, while running the same programs year after year may make members happy and comfortable, a true leader will occasionally pause and ask if the programs are potentially distracting them from their real mission. For example, is the annual Christmas program still effective in helping fulfill the Great Commission? If not, then tradition and love for the program must be set aside for something new.

Nowadays, many Christians seem intent to voice their political interests and affiliations. Being involved in politics can be a sign of healthy concern for the community at large, but political activity has also been used by the enemy as a distraction. Satan has many convinced that our answers are found in political parties, not Christ. While Christian nationalism seems to be gaining popularity, this was never on Jesus' agenda.

In conjunction with this lie, Christians may be found distracted with non-essential issues that do not move the kingdom of God forward. Again, the essentials are—relationship with Christ, sharing the gospel, and making disciples. Putting one's full energy into supporting political parties that may establish favorable legislation does not fall into these categories.

We must ask if such actions (e.g., always teaching but never learning, maintaining popular but ineffective programs, promoting politicians) are merely a sign of selfish baserunning. In other words, sometimes we put what we want ahead of the good of the team. But Jesus has already established what must be done for the good of the kingdom, and he does not need the rogue baserunner trying to heroically win the game by himself. Our Lord is looking for followers who are in relationship with him, and thus, are striving to fulfill kingdom objectives.

THE WRAP-UP

Someone once said, "Starve your distractions, feed your focus." As we navigate the busyness of our world today, that's good advice to remember. Think about it—loss of focus makes everything blurry. And when things are blurry, we can't see properly.

I'm reminded of the old cartoon "Mr. Magoo." The cartoon first aired in 1949 and was voiced by Jim Backus (he was also millionaire Thurston Howell III on *Gilligan's Island*). Mr. Magoo had extreme near-sightedness and because he refused to wear glasses, he was always lost and putting himself in dangerous (and comical) situations.

Loss of focus will do that to you. And while it may be comical in a cartoon, it's not a laughing matter with regard to the Christian life. Thus, we must be on the alert and keep our eyes focused on the things that matter most. It's only then that we see things as we really should.

CHAPTER 4

Caught Leaning

ON JULY 27, 2016, former Cy Young Award winner[75] R.A. Dickey was on the hill for the Toronto Blue Jays versus the San Diego Padres. In the top of the first inning, Dickey struck out leadoff batter Travis Jankowski but then proceeded to walk Wil Myers. Clearly wanting to steal second base, Myers began leaning toward second, when the right-handed Dickey spun toward first base to promptly pick him off.[76] The pickoff was a sign of things to come, as Dickey also had the last laugh that day, getting the win despite giving up six earned runs in just 5.2 innings pitched. Myers managed two walks but wore the collar by going hitless in three at bats.

You can often tell when there's an anxious baserunner who really wants to steal a base. They get up on their toes, their hands will drop toward the inside of their knees, their fingers often move like that of a pianist, and their eyes are in deep concentration on the pitcher. Wanting desperately to get moving, sometimes they try to cheat a bit by transferring some weight toward second base.

Successful pickoffs are often the result of catching a guy leaning. With the baserunner's weight moving away from the base, a savvy pitcher can wheel and deliver a throw that can easily beat the runner back. I've always thought that getting caught leaning is almost as inexcusable as getting caught sleeping. If you need to lean and cheat a bit to steal second base, you should re-evaluate why you're trying to steal in the first place. In other words, leave the base thefts to the guys who can really motor.

"Guessing and going" is a similar way guys get picked off. Because few players are true speedsters, some coaches teach players to simply gamble on the pitcher not throwing over to first base. Thus, instead of waiting for the pitcher to commit to deliver a pitch home, on the first sign of pitcher movement, the runner bolts for second base. There is no use of caution here, no assurance that the pitcher is committed to throwing home. The runner simply sees the pitcher move and almost simultaneously runs. If you guess wrong, you're easy prey.

PRAYING BEFORE MOVING

In the church, it's far too common to encounter "prayer time" that is something like 90 percent talking about prayer needs and a mere 10 percent of actual prayer—and at times, that's a very generous estimate. Now think about that for a minute. We sometimes have special meetings that are specifically set aside for prayer, and yet, we spend a disproportionate amount of time talking to one another, instead of to God.

These experiences reveal several possible problems. Perhaps we feel like we don't know how to pray, that we don't want to pray, that we don't like public prayer, that we get bored in prayer, or that we don't value prayer because we're not convinced it really matters. Regardless, it's clear that something is wrong.

Unfortunately, church leadership meetings are often no better. Many can attest to attending three-hour meetings that conclude with a one-minute prayer for God's blessing. This backward meeting model is reminiscent of leaning baserunners. Instead of seeking God's will, by spending ten to fifteen minutes in prayer at the outset of the meeting, hours of discussion are potentially wasted as God's direction was never sought first. Instead, church leaders just decide where they want to go and start leaning toward action. Then afterward, they ask God to bless what they have decided.

THE PICKOFF

When we hear Christians contemplate why the church seems powerless and ineffective in today's world, we should always ask if our decisions are being guided along by the Holy Spirit in prayer, or if we're guilty of getting ahead of God on the basepaths. Fruitless ministry is often a result of the latter.

The sad truth is that I was tempted to forge ahead in completing this chapter without first asking the Lord to direct my thoughts. That is a horrible habit influenced by a culture that promotes self-sufficiency and immediate satisfaction. While leaning baserunners are antsy and impatient, we must learn to be patient as we seek God prior to acting.

When we continually fail to pray before moving, we should stop and examine our relationship with Christ.

When we continually fail to pray before moving, we should stop and examine our relationship with Christ. Could our eagerness to move forward without praying show a lack of trust in God? Or worse yet, could it be an indication that our relationship with God is suffering?

The first twelve verses of Proverbs 3 essentially remind us to keep God first, and to obey and trust him so we will be blessed. While many are familiar with verses 5–6 (a couplet[77] that belongs together), these verses should probably be seen in tandem with verses 7–8.[78]

The passage says, ⁵ "Trust in the Lord with all your heart and do not lean on your own understanding. ⁶ In all your ways acknowledge Him, and He will make your paths straight. ⁷ Do not be wise in your own eyes; fear the Lord and turn away from evil. ⁸ It will be healing to your body and refreshment to your bones."

This speaks into our culture and reminds us that the solutions we devise often result from our inflated egos, as we sometimes believe we are wise enough to make the right decisions on our own. Again, we erroneously think we are self-sufficient.

Caught Leaning

But the proverb reminds us that Christ followers must "trust," "acknowledge," and "fear" God, not "leaning on our own understanding" or being "wise in our own eyes." When we do these things, then God will make our "paths straight." Living within the will of God is such a powerful blessing that it's like a "refreshment" for us. It brings vitality to us and helps us think straight.

Leaning into action before first consulting God can have dire circumstances. The book of Joshua opens with these words,

> ¹ Now it came about after the death of Moses the servant of the Lord, that the Lord spoke to Joshua the son of Nun, Moses' servant, saying, ² "Moses My servant is dead; so now arise, cross this Jordan, you and all this people, to the land which I am giving to them, to the sons of Israel. ³ Every place on which the sole of your foot steps, I have given it to you, just as I spoke to Moses. ⁴ From the wilderness and this Lebanon, even as far as the great river, the river Euphrates, all the land of the Hittites, and as far as the Great Sea toward the setting of the sun will be your territory. ⁵ No one will *be able to* oppose you all the days of your life. Just as I have been with Moses, I will be with you; I will not desert you nor abandon you.[79]

Soon afterward, Joshua led the people over the Jordan River and into the Promised Land. Chapters 6 and 8 tell of Israel conquering the cities of Jericho and Ai. After hearing of these conquests, five kings from the surrounding area decide to join forces in the fight against Israel.[80]

But the leaders from Gibeon decided on another course of action, choosing instead to seek peace with Joshua by using proactive deception.[81] They pretended to be travelers from a 'far country" who had recently heard of Israel's reputation. Thus, in fear they proclaim that they will be Israel's "servants" and ask them to make a "covenant" with them.

Joshua 9:14–15 tell us of Joshua's decision. It says, 14 "So the men *of Israel* took some of their provisions, and did not ask the counsel of the Lord. 15 And Joshua made peace with them and

The Pickoff

made a covenant with them, to let them live; and the leaders of the congregation swore *an oath* to them." Just a short three days later, the Israelites learned the truth—that the Gibeonites were neighbors already living in the land. Because they swore an oath before the Lord, Israel kept their word and let them live.

Because Joshua did not consult God, Israel made an ill-advised covenant and failed to completely drive out all the heathen nations. Joshua should have known to be careful, as Deuteronomy 7 provided clear instruction, and even the reasons for them. It says,

> **1** When the Lord your God brings you into the land where you are entering to take possession of it, and He drives away many nations from before you, the Hittites, the Girgashites, the Amorites, the Canaanites, the Perizzites, the Hivites, and the Jebusites, seven nations greater and mightier than you, **2** and when the Lord your God turns them over to you and you defeat them, you shall utterly destroy them. You shall not make a covenant with them nor be gracious to them. **3** Furthermore, you shall not intermarry with them: you shall not give your daughters to their sons, nor shall you take their daughters for your sons. 4 For they will turn your sons away from following Me, and they will serve other gods; then the anger of the Lord will be kindled against you and He will quickly destroy you. **5** But this is what you shall do to them: you shall tear down their altars, smash their memorial stones, cut their Asherim to pieces, and burn their carved images in the fire. **6** For you are a holy people to the Lord your God; the Lord your God has chosen you to be a people for His personal possession out of all the peoples who are on the face of the earth.

By failing to consult God, Joshua was foolish and made a covenant with the very people who could persuade them to forsake God. In fact, Gibeon was one of the Hivite cities,[82] who are specifically mentioned here in Deuteronomy 7:1. And the peace treaty was more impactful than one might think, as it included the cities of "Gibeon, Chephirah, Beeroth, and Kiriath-jearim."[83]

The establishment of this covenant had consequences. Notable is that Saul broke the covenant and tried to annihilate the Gibeonites.[84] As a result, the Lord sent a famine that lasted for three years. After God revealed the cause of the famine to David, the king made amends with the Gibeonites by giving seven of Saul's descendants over to be hanged, a retribution for the violation.

By failing to stop and seek God's will, violations were committed, and people were killed. It's an ugly story that teaches an important lesson—we must pray before moving.

Another biblical example comes from the life of King Asa, the third king of Judah who reigned from approximately 910–839 BC. He was one of the good kings and the Bible says,

> [11] Now Asa did what was right in the sight of the Lord, like his father David. [12] He also removed the male cult prostitutes from the land and removed all the idols which his fathers had made. [13] And even his mother Maacah, he also removed her from *the position of* queen mother, because she had made an abominable image as an Asherah; and Asa cut down her abominable image and burned *it* at the brook Kidron. [14] But the high places were not eliminated; nevertheless Asa's heart was wholly devoted to the Lord all his days. [15] And he brought into the house of the Lord the holy gifts of his father and his own holy gifts: silver, gold, and *valuable* utensils (1 Kgs 15:11–15).

One blemish of Asa's record, however, comes at the end of his life. Second Chronicles 16 says, [12] "In the thirty-ninth year of his reign Asa became diseased in his feet. His disease was severe, yet even in his disease he did not seek the Lord, but the physicians. [13] So Asa lay down with his fathers, and died in the forty-first year of his reign."

Asa's first, and only, response to illness was to seek physicians. The physicians were unable to help, so he died. Since the writer makes note of this detail, we're left to believe that if he had sought the Lord, he would have been healed. Thus, some translations like the NASB begin verse 13 with the word, "So." This is quite a sad ending for such a great king. Instead of being cleared to run the bases, King Asa suffered the ultimate pickoff.

Christians are often tempted to run ahead of God. When this happens, we take out bad loans (e.g., a vehicle we can't really afford), take the wrong job, overuse credit cards, make commitments we can't keep, date the wrong people, and church hop. Like Joshua, we can all readily admit that our failure to pray has led to poor decision-making.

Satan claims victory when we move without seeking the Lord, as such movement serves to prove that we trust in ourselves. Such movement also demonstrates a selfish nature that must grasp for things that bring instant gratification. There can be no doubt that Satan loves to pick off Christian baserunners who continually get caught leaning.

We must also learn from Asa, for in his example we are reminded that failure to pray sometimes leads to God's inaction. Our failure to pray stifles the activity of the Holy Spirit who wants to speak into our lives and provide clarity. In prayer, we will even find the Holy Spirit challenging our faith by telling us we can do what does not seem possible.

The enemy will do anything to distract us from prayer. He will tell us, "Prayer makes no difference, it doesn't move God, and God certainly doesn't speak to you." In getting us to bite on any of these lies, Satan sets us up to be another casualty on the basepaths.

PRAYER KEEPS US GROUNDED

Our struggle to grasp the importance of prayer and remain steady in it is a bit curious. For prayer is one of the very things that keeps us grounded in our faith. Let me illustrate with the following four scenarios.

In the first scenario, a group of Christians have laborious conversations and decide to plant a new church. And let's say that the decision seems successful, in that the church begins to grow. While it's difficult for us to see this as a poor decision, God may actually view it this way. This is because the church leaders failed to seek God's guidance in this decision, and God knew this was not a wise decision.

The group didn't see the future consequences of this action. They didn't have the proper infrastructure in place to properly assimilate and disciple these new church attenders. In the end, many of these visitors leave the church and don't view it as a place that actually impacted their lives. As time passes, the church eventually closes.

The second scenario is similar except everything is going well. Thus, we may never stop to question the wisdom of this decision. The problem, as previously stated, is that leaning into action without first praying for God's direction can enhance our belief in self-sufficiency (whether it be implicit or explicit). For sake of argument, we will assume that these church leaders love God, and that in his graciousness God blessed the decision. But what can't be lost on us is that such action (moving without praying) will eventually be repeated. Why wouldn't it be?

And God will simply not continue to bless decision-making that fails to seek his guidance. This second, and seemingly successful scenario, does not properly ground the Christian. For when self-directed decision-making continues, it is bound to fail. And when it fails, it sometimes leaves the decision-maker disillusioned. That is when Satan jumps in and tells the believer, "Maybe this Jesus stuff isn't exactly what you thought it was. Look at how disastrous that decision was. God doesn't care what you are doing. In fact, maybe there is no God, anyway. Just look at the proof. You're working your tail off for Jesus, but there's no blessing."

A third scenario begins with the church leaders praying before even discussing any future plans. God leads them along and everything turns out well. This is clearly the scenario we would all like to see.

But there's a fourth scenario, a development we don't like to discuss. The church leaders pray before discussing any future action. In fact, they are fully convinced that God has spoken to them about their plans. They move out in faith, but things never quite work out as they had hoped. It leaves the leaders frustrated, sad, and at times, causes them to question God.

Just like the second scenario, the enemy will try to take advantage of this situation. He will try to convince the leaders that they never heard from God. He'll say, "All of this Holy Spirit speaking stuff is just nonsense. God doesn't speak, and even if he does, he certainly never spoke to you. Just go back to reading your Bible, but don't bother praying anymore. You'll find comfort in those pages. But just forget this 'asking' and 'expecting big things' drivel. Those are nice thoughts, but let's face the facts, you're nobody special. Just do your devotions and be faithful in service."

See, if he must, the enemy will settle for us burying ourselves in Bible study, as long as we are not prompted to action. Faith must be moved out of the pages of the text and appropriated into our lives. It's never enough to simply believe, as even the demons believe.[85] Faith must always be put into action, as we must become "doers of the word."[86]

We should pray before moving, and not just for clarity and wisdom. We should pray because prayer prompts movement—the type of movement that God blesses. This is because prayer leads to hearing (a hearing based on things we have already learned in God's word), and hearing leads to obedience. When God asks us to move and we move, we will be blessed.

But now you say, "Scenario four did not paint a picture of blessing. So, how can it be that action promoted by prayer always leads to blessing?" The fact is simple, when God speaks and we obey, the blessing of God is not dependent on what we may call "viewable blessings."

Just consider Hebrews 11, what is often called "The Faith Chapter." Here, biblical heroes are paraded in front of us as a "great cloud of witnesses" to encourage us to "run with endurance the race that is set before us."[87] Yet, these men and women are not applauded for accomplishments always seen in their lifetime. Instead, they are recognized for living by faith, which is the "certainty of things hoped for, a proof of things not seen."[88]

See, the blessing of God is not dependent on our alleged accomplishments—the blessing of God is based on obedience (faith in action). After discussing Abraham, Sarah, Isaac, and Jacob, the writer makes an insightful statement that should not escape our notice. Hebrews 11:13 says, "All these died in faith, without receiving the promises, but having seen and welcomed them from a distance, and having confessed that they were strangers and exiles on the earth."

In today's megachurch and "bless me" culture, we sometimes fall into the trap of believing that the greatest of God's servants must be prolific leaders as evidenced by their "success." In fact, due to a lack of credentials and accomplishments, if Abraham were alive today, he would never be asked to speak at a church conference. Nevertheless, the Apostle Paul called this man "the father of all who believe."[89]

Hebrews 11:35–38 winds down the chapter by recounting heroes of the faith who were tortured, mocked, flogged, imprisoned, stoned, sawn in two, killed by the sword, afflicted, and tormented. Others were reduced to wandering in deserts, living in caves, and even finding shelter in holes in the ground. And remarkably, the chapter concludes with these words "And all these, having gained approval through their faith, did not receive what was promised, because God had provided something better for us, so that apart from us they would not be made perfect."[90]

The message is clear—blessing is not always seen in this lifetime. As Leonard Sweet says, "Jesus humans start and support ministries whose benefits and blessings they will never get to see or taste its fruit."[91] Knowing this fact is comforting, and yet living in this reality can be very difficult. We must now return to scenario four, as these leaders were convinced they heard from God, and yet the ambitious plans did not work out. Should we conclude that they were mistaken? The answer is, "No."

See, it's this "hearing" from God that keeps the Christian grounded. It kept Abraham, Sarah, Isaac, and Jacob grounded. Likewise, it will keep us grounded. Satan will work to make us question our relationship with Christ. But we must never forget that Jesus says his sheep know his voice.[92] Admittedly, hearing the voice of God with absolute clarity seems rare and at times we find ourselves feeling uncertain. Nevertheless, unpleasant results (what some may call "failures") should not be the driving factor for assessing blessing.

In scenario one, God did not bless the zealous actions of those who failed to seek him, and this is what we may expect. Yet because God is gracious, in scenario two, God blessed the action of zealous Christians who failed to pray. Still, such action is foolish and should never be repeated. In fact, such repeated action will eventually result in scenario one.

In scenario three, we could see that God blessed the actions of those who sought him in prayer before moving to action, and this is what we expect (what we think is probably most normal). Yet, in scenario four we could not see how God blessed those actions. Nevertheless, when God speaks and we obey, blessing is bound to follow. We may never understand how God used our obedience to bless others, nor may we ever understand how our obedience impacted our personal growth and relationship with our Lord. But obedience to God always leads to blessing, and it matters little what others think of the visible results.

Again, it's the combination of hearing and obeying that keeps one grounded. As Moses prepared the Israelites to take possession of the Promised Land, he advised them to keep the statutes taught to them. In his urging in Deuteronomy 4, Moses told them to not forget the things their eyes had seen, nor how the Lord spoke to them "from the midst of the fire." After God gave the Ten Commandments, their response was to "perform" (to "do" them).

The lesson here is that we must not forget what we have seen and/or heard from God. These things keep us grounded in our faith. When life throws us a curve, we must return to those moments of "seeing" and "hearing," as they strengthen our faith and serve to reinforce the relationship we have with our Lord. If we will hold steadfast in remembering the action of God, our commitment and endurance to our Lord can remain steady.

Satan will vigorously work to make us question what we have seen and heard, as he is looking to pick off baserunners who can advance the kingdom of God. But we must always remember that we walk by faith. And while seeing and hearing may be rare, it must be enough. Hebrews 11:6 says, "Without faith it is impossible to please *Him*, for the one who comes to God must believe that He exists, and *that* He proves to be One who rewards those who seek Him."

THE WRAP-UP

In the 1997 political satire, *Wag the Dog*, Robert De Niro's character Conrad Brean says, "A good plan today is better than a perfect plan tomorrow." Unfortunately, many Christians live by the same motto, as we prefer jumping into action over waiting on God in prayer. Whether it's our impatience or our lack of certainty in recognizing God's voice that moves us forward without God, one thing is for sure—smart baserunners shouldn't get caught leaning.

We must dismiss the notion that our plan today without God is good enough, as it never is. Jumping into motion may enable a baserunner to pick up the occasional stolen base (on one's own strength) but waiting on God always guarantees the perfect result that God intends. The difference between self-initiated motion and God-initiated motion is the difference between "our will" and "his will," and we all know which one is best.

CHAPTER 5

Bad Advice

J. C. WAS ONE of the toughest kids I knew, and he'd turn out to be a great high school football player. The irony is that, as tough as he was, he was afraid of a baseball. So, it was completely understandable that he never wanted to play organized baseball. Being one of our best friends, however, several of us were able to talk him into joining our team during the summer following eighth grade.

Because J. C. had no baseball experience but was so fast, the coach primarily used him as a pinch runner. J. C. came to mind as I was preparing for this chapter because I could imagine the scenario I will be presenting happening to a novice player such as him. And while my memory does not allow me to be certain whether the following did in fact happen to J. C., I do know with certainty that I've seen it happen.

As a timid runner hugs the base too closely, the first base coach immediately starts encouraging them by saying, "Get off, get off farther. Take another step." And then it happens almost as the coach is in mid-sentence. The pitcher throws over and picks the runner off first base.

While the majority of pickoffs are the result of skilled pitchers or faulty baserunning, sometimes it's the result of bad coaching. Occasionally, you'll get an over-zealous first base coach who keeps insisting that his player get a bigger lead. I can tell you from experience that some players need this encouragement. However, sometimes the coach simply gets it wrong and is guilty of giving out bad advice to an inexperienced baserunner.

LISTENING TO THE WRONG VOICES

Thanks to information technology, the world bombards us with opinion after opinion, as a sea of humanity strives to persuade us to adhere to their message. The enemy must enjoy this continual onslaught, as arrogance and hatred seem to gain a great deal of traction in our clickbait culture.

It's important that we listen to the right voices and, as we may expect, the Bible has a great deal to say on this topic. For example, the Apostle Paul wrote thirteen letters and in each of them he provides invaluable advice about the type of voices we should or shouldn't listen to. The following surveys each of his letters and explores Paul's concern for Christian baserunners.

Romans—The Sinful Voice from Within

In Romans 6, Paul tells us that before we were "freed from sin" (6:7, 18, 22) by the work of Christ, we were "slaves to sin" (6:6, 17, 20). He elaborates on the power of sin in the next chapter by discussing his own internal struggle, as he desires to do good but his sinful nature fights against that desire. Paul even confesses that sometimes he does the very things he doesn't want to do, and that the flesh seems to win the raging battle within him.[93]

The apostle continues in chapter 8,[94] however, by proclaiming that there is no condemnation for those who are in Christ. After all, Christ has paid the price and has set us free. But again, Paul returns to the power of sin and reminds us of our weakness. Thus, he advises us to set our minds on the things of the Spirit, and not on things of the flesh. We must remember, "the mind set on the flesh is hostile toward God." But praise be to God, the Holy Spirit helps us in our weakness and Christ intercedes for us. Thus, we are conquerors, as nothing can separate us from the love of God.

The lesson here is that sin is a powerful combatant and remains, so to speak, as a voice from within that wages war with our spiritual man. This is an important truth, as we live in a culture that often says things like, "Follow your gut," "Listen to your heart," or "Trust your instincts." The danger of believing these slogans lies in the fact that sometimes our instincts guide us well, and sometimes they don't. We must remember that sin corrupts even the conscience, causing us to listen to a heart persuaded by selfish motives.

Thus, we readily believe lies such as, "Just be a good person and do what you need to do to be happy." One can almost sense the enemy whispering in our ear, echoing such nonsense. Doing what makes us happy is sometimes self-serving, and it's laughable to think we're being good people when we live selfishly. Paul's words here in Romans serve as a powerful reminder to us. If we want to continue safely running the basepaths, we must deny the sinful voice that lies within.

1 Corinthians—Voices of Worldly Wisdom

To say the church at Corinth had its problems is a gross understatement. In fact, in 1 Corinthians, Paul addresses "at least eleven different concerns, ten of which are behavioral."[95] Among their many problems is that they had an inflated sense of self-importance. Specifically, they seemed to believe they were super spiritual, the result of being endowed with "special wisdom and superior knowledge."[96]

The Corinthians even brought out a sarcastic[97] streak in Paul, as he spoke of their alleged superiority, strength, and honor. They see themselves as "having arrived," and in no need of the apostles.[98] But Paul warns them against being deceived. He says, "If anyone among you thinks that he is wise in this age, he must become foolish, so that he may become wise. For the wisdom of this world is foolishness in the sight of God."[99] Paul recognized that the Christians at Corinth had become victims to the voices of worldly wisdom.

BAD ADVICE

"Wisdom" can come from many sources. It can be the result of spiritual experience, scientific method, philosophical theory, education, and even maturity. When a person becomes wise in their own eyes, it often seems impossible to speak the truth of Christ into their lives. Paul reminds us that, when not checked against the ultimate wisdom of God, the voices of wisdom are futile. It's only when we look to Christ that we will find true wisdom.[100]

In seeking to help them get their eyes back on Christ, Paul urges them to "imitate" him, as he imitates Christ.[101] This is a common approach of Paul's, as he often encourages others to follow in his example.[102] Thus, we see Paul attempting to counter the voices of worldly wisdom by having them focus on the gospel he proclaims, one which comes in "demonstration of the Spirit and of power."[103]

2 Corinthians—Voices Who Rely on the Flesh

As Paul writes this letter, he "attempts to repair damaged relationships, encourage participation in an offering for Christians in Jerusalem, and also deal with the so-called 'super apostles' who are undermining his ministry."[104] Paul blasts these false apostles that he sarcastically refers to as "eminent apostles."[105]

In calling them false apostles, Paul elaborates[106] and says they are "deceitful workers, disguising themselves as apostles of Christ." They have been so effective in their deception that it's no wonder Paul reminds them that "even Satan disguises himself as an angel of light."[107] And while they masquerade as "servants of righteousness," they will be judged accordingly.

Paul provides us with tremendous insight when he also notes how "many boast according to the flesh."[108] Baker says, "Clues from 2 Corinthians indicate they were proud of their Jewish heritage (11:22), their Christian' service (11:23), their oratorical skill (11:6), their self-confidence (1:15–17), and their charismatic experiences (12:12)."[109] Regardless of these accomplishments of the flesh, "They preached a different gospel than Paul's.[110] They also accepted money from the Corinthians, unlike Paul who refused it (12:16)."[111]

Considering how Paul's first letter to the Corinthians revealed the Christians there had an inflated sense of self, believing their wisdom made them spiritual giants, it's not shocking they later became prey to false teachers who also exaggerated their personal greatness. We'd be mistaken to identify these voices as merely being false teachers. Specifically, they were voices who relied on the flesh.

The "super apostles" had no need to rely upon God, they already had their act together. They had the right heritage, they did good Christian things, and they were slick talkers. Jesus' words in Matthew 7:15–23 come to mind, as Jesus pulls the curtain back on such people who call him "Lord" and do good deeds in his name but display unhealthy fruit that exposes them for what they are—impostors.

We live in a world that pushes "successful" Christians into the spotlight. Yet, worldly success is not always the result of a healthy Christian life. Success is often achieved through works of flesh that, in and of themselves, prove nothing at all about one's spirituality. As Christ-followers, we must do just that—follow Christ. Voices that rely on the power of the flesh may have great influence, but we must remain steady in our examination of fruit so that we can ensure we are listening to the right voices.

Galatians—Voices of Legalism

After providing a customary greeting at the outset, Paul quickly moves into his purpose for writing to the churches at Galatia. He says, "I am amazed that you are so quickly deserting Him who called you by the grace of Christ, for a different gospel, which is not *just* another *account*; but there are some who are disturbing you and want to distort the gospel of Christ."[112]

This distorted "gospel" was a product of Jewish false teachers we call Judaizers. They taught that following Jesus was fine, as long as one remained a good Jew. Of course, being a good Jew meant that one must adhere to the Jewish laws. Thus, this perverted message attempted to blend faith in Christ with good works, and Paul would have none of that.

Paul says, "You foolish Galatians, who has bewitched you, before whose eyes Jesus Christ was publicly portrayed *as* crucified? This is the only thing I want to find out from you: did you receive the Spirit by works of the Law, or by hearing with faith? Are you so foolish? Having begun by the Spirit, are you now being perfected by the flesh?"[113]

Later, Paul asks, "How is it that you turn back again to the weak and worthless elementary principles, to which you want to be enslaved all over again?"[114] Paul sums up his argument well in that single statement, as attempting to obtain salvation by works simply leads to enslavement. And that's exactly where the voices of legalism always send a person—toward bondage.

Legalism says, "Do this and don't do that. Follow the rules and gain favor with God." But as Paul says, "It was for freedom that Christ set us free; therefore keep standing firm and do not be subject again to a yoke of slavery."[115] The Gospel message is so incredibly generous, that at times we may be tempted to think pleasing God can't be as easy as it sounds. But it is, and we must toss the voices of legalism to the side and run the basepaths with faith.

Ephesians—Spiritual Voices

Of all of Paul's letters, Ephesians is the most general and the least situational. In fact, no particular problems are addressed—perhaps that's why this letter is so refreshing! It's been called "the crown of St. Paul's writings" and is definitely a fan favorite. In Ephesians we read that Christ-followers are "blessed, chosen, and predestined as sons and daughters in Christ." They are called "saints, children of light, and holy." And they are told that they are "a new creation, redeemed, forgiven, and reconciled to Christ." What's not to love about Ephesians?

Yet, as Paul begins to conclude the letter, the tone slightly changes.[116] He encourages us "to stand firm against the schemes of the devil . . . against the rulers, against the powers, against the world forces of this darkness, against the spiritual *forces* of wickedness in the heavenly *places*."

While we've already discussed this text in length, it's important to note that spiritual voices surround us. Some are scheming against us, but the Holy Spirit wants to speak life into our beings. We must be on the "alert," as forces of darkness look to pick us off the basepaths. By listening to the Spirit, we will "persevere."

Philippians—Voices that Agitate

While the topic of unity runs as a thread through this short letter,[117] the most prominent theme that gains our attention is that we should "rejoice" (9x) and have "joy" (7x). Amazingly, Paul makes this declaration while being imprisoned. But Paul's primary concern is not for himself, but for the Christians at Philippi. He writes to encourage them, as opposition to the gospel remains a threat to their safety on the basepaths.

Paul's concerns are many, as he refers to "opponents," Judaizers, and "enemies of the cross of Christ."[118] He also mentions some who preach Christ "from envy and strife" and "selfish ambition."[119] Unfortunately, it seems unlikely that all of these refer to the same group of people, showing the severity of the problem.

Of particular interest is Philippians 1:15-17. Paul says, "Some, to be sure, are preaching Christ even from envy and strife, but some also from goodwill; the latter *do it* out of love, knowing that I am appointed for the defense of the gospel; the former proclaim Christ out of selfish ambition rather than from pure motives, thinking that they are causing me distress in my imprisonment."

Some translations render the word "strife" (v. 15) as "rivalry" (e.g., ESV, NIV). And while the Greek word means "strife, discord, or contention,"[120] pairing the term with "envy" may lend to a contextual decision to help clarify exactly what Paul meant. Thus, some translators see Paul as referring to some who are envious of him, even seeing him as a rival. Fee agrees and says, "In our text these words express the underlying reason for the newfound boldness of some, which, of course, can only have been directed at Paul personally. Jealousy is one of the basest expressions of human fallenness."[121]

These rivals who enjoy creating misery for others can be thought of as voices that agitate. Sadly, because we live in a world where agitators daily make headline news, we are all too familiar with these voices. They invade our social media posts, our casual conversations, and at times seem bent on zapping the joy out of life. Agitators make a person want to retreat into safe but lonely places. In doing so, they invade healthy relationships, destroying community.

Agitating voices are one of the reasons Paul addresses unity. So, the apostle tells us to "stand firm," "strive together," and to represent Christ well. By not giving the agitating voices the attention they desire, we can work together as a team that is ensured victory.

Colossians—Voices of Philosophical Emptiness

I love Colossians. First, it's a mini-Ephesians, in that about a third of the Colossian material is found in Ephesians. Second, Colossians 1:15–20 contains one of the greatest Christological sections of the New Testament. And third, I love the practical nature of chapters 3–4. But interrupting this beautiful letter is chapter 2, a section where Paul addresses what some scholars have called, "The Colossian Heresy."

Colossians 2:8 is key, as Paul says, "See to it that there is no one who takes you captive through philosophy and empty deception in accordance with human tradition, in accordance with the elementary principles of the world, rather than in accordance with Christ." With this in mind, it's of no surprise that "the words 'wisdom' (6x) and 'knowledge' (5x) are often repeated, sometimes together.[122] Paul tells the Colossians they must have a 'true knowledge'[123] of God that comes from knowing Christ."[124]

The Colossian church was invaded by a strange mixture of Gentile and Jewish teaching,[125] which created a conceit in some. Some of the practices of these false teachers had an "appearance of wisdom," but ultimately were of "no value against fleshly indulgence."

In our quest to gain enlightenment, wisdom, and/or happiness, we often listen to the worldly voices of philosophy. But we must be careful of listening to such voices, as they only entrench us in sin, doing nothing to truly set us free. To the contrary, these deceptive voices only leave us empty. But praise be to God, Christ can make us "full" (or "complete").[126]

deceptive voices only leave us empty

1 & 2 Thessalonians—Voices of Hatred

During his second missionary journey, Paul spent several weeks at Thessalonica and established a church.[127] Thus, it's not surprising that the first letter has a very personal tone. He clearly has a great affection for the Christians here (e.g., the word "brethren" is used 18x) and he often applauds them for their commitment to Christ (e.g., the phrase "your faith" is used 7x). In fact, Paul states that they have become "imitators"[128] of the apostles and of the churches in Judea. In doing so, they became an "example" to other believers.[129]

When reading this letter, one can sense the pride Paul has in them. Speaking on behalf of Silas and Timothy, Paul says, "We also constantly thank God that when you received the word of God which you heard from us, you accepted *it* not *as* the word of *mere* men, but as what it really is, the word of God, which also is at work in you who believe."[130] Thus, as they continued to follow Christ in faith, Paul wrote this letter of encouragement to them—and they needed it.

"The encouragement, in part, stems from persecution which must be endured (note the various words: tribulation, suffering, mistreated, opposition, hostile, and affliction—1:6; 2:2, 14–15; 3:3–4, 7)."[131] It's no wonder that as Paul begins to conclude the first letter, he says, "See that no one repays another with evil for evil, but always seek what is good for one another and for all people."[132]

BAD ADVICE

Just as Paul had endured voices of hatred,[133] the Christians at Thessalonica had to do the same.[134] There will always be those who are hostile to messengers of the gospel, doing what they can to prevent the spreading of the life-saving message.[135] We must not allow the voices of hatred to stall kingdom work. Instead, we must forge ahead and imitate the faithful that have come before us, setting an example to future servants of Christ.

As persecution persists, Paul writes a second letter to encourage the Christians at Thessalonica. In reaffirming their perseverance and faith,[136] he urges them to "hold on" to the things they have been taught.[137]

Whereas in the first letter Paul asked the Christians to resist revenge against those who harm them,[138] in this second letter Paul sets out to comfort them by reminding them of God's comfort and impending judgment against the voices of hatred that are bent on persecuting Christ-followers. Paul had briefly mentioned God's "wrath" against such evildoers in 1 Thessalonians 2:16, but now he spends considerable time in telling the persecuted that God is aware of their hardship, and that he will have the final say in this matter.

> Paul says, *"This is* a plain indication of God's righteous judgment so that you will be considered worthy of the kingdom of God, for which you indeed are suffering. For after all it is *only* right for God to repay with affliction those who afflict you, and *to give* relief to you who are afflicted, *along* with us, when the Lord Jesus will be revealed from heaven with His mighty angels in flaming fire, dealing out retribution to those who do not know God, and to those who do not obey the gospel of our Lord Jesus. These people will pay the penalty of eternal destruction, away from the presence of the Lord and from the glory of His power, when He comes to be glorified among His saints on that day, and to be marveled at among all who have believed—because our testimony to you was believed (2 Thess 1:5-10).

In these letters to the Christians at Thessalonica, we are reminded that the voices of hatred do not escape God's attention.

THE PICKOFF

He is aware of those who oppose the gospel, some who are even bent on harming his faithful servants. We are not to cower down to opposition, as to be picked off base. To faithfully run the bases, we must take comfort in knowing that our God is in control, and that his servants will be rewarded in their steadfastness to Christ.

1 Timothy, Titus, and 2 Timothy—Noises of Nonsense

Combatting the false teaching at Ephesus is forefront in the first letter to Timothy. "Not only is this a prevalent theme throughout, but the letter both begins and ends[139] with the topic. It's of no surprise that Paul often mentions 'teaching, teachers, teach' (11x), sometimes referring to the need for sound teaching."[140]

In examining the aforementioned passages, some key descriptions about these false teachers surface. Their teaching involves "useless speculation," "fruitless discussion," "controversial questions and disputes," and "empty chatter."[141] In their great "knowledge,"[142] these false teachers make "confident assertions" but understand nothing.[143] Most importantly, they do not teach the sound words of Christ that conform to godliness.[144]

Since it's clear that these teachers love to hear themselves talk, and yet have nothing of substance that deserves attention, we may diverge from our aforementioned "voices" title. In this case, these teachers may appropriately be called "Noises of Nonsense."

And yet for all of their useless teaching, they have managed to pick runners off base. Paul reveals that some have now "wandered from the faith."[145] Thus, Paul encourages Christian baserunners to "fight the good fight of faith"[146] and to press on in Christ.

While the noises of nonsense teach us that talk is cheap, Paul continually drives home the importance of "godliness."[147] And, of course, godliness speaks to actions of the believer, something much greater than mere lip service that may or may not be supported by evidence.

Godliness is key in this letter, and "it must be understood within the framework of our witness, the most repeated theme of the letter. In fact, reference to the Christian witness is found within every chapter of the letter."[148] Because godliness and the Christian witness work hand in hand, Paul sees godly behavior as imperative. We must keep in mind, it's the godly Christian witness that points others toward Jesus. Furthermore, godliness keeps one safe on the basepaths and reminds the baserunner to simply mute the noises of nonsense.

Titus is in Crete,[149] an island about 230 miles south of Ephesus. And yet, this letter sounds very similar to 1 Timothy. The noises of nonsense are being heard at Crete, as Paul speaks of "empty talkers and deceivers," "myths," and "foolish controversies and genealogies and strife and disputes" which are "useless and worthless."[150] And like the teachers at Ephesus, some were clearly Jewish teachers who had lost their way.[151] Furthermore, Paul describes their motives as disgraceful, saying they taught a form of godliness that was merely for dishonest gain.[152]

And again, as in 1 Timothy, Paul speaks of the necessity of godly living.[153] However, his emphasis in this letter is "good deeds" (used 6x).[154] Paul says that while the false teachers profess to know God, their deeds tell quite another story, being found as "detestable" and "worthless."[155] The reminder is clear—it's not what we say, it's what we do that proves who we really are. Successful baserunners must filter out worthless noise that is unsupported by good deeds, and personally "engage in good deeds."[156]

While Paul's second letter to Timothy does not explicitly state that Timothy is still in Ephesus, the evidence strongly suggests such. First, as Paul describes the false teaching in both letters, there is a remarkable similarity in his choice of words. He speaks of "disputes about words,"[157] "worldly and empty chatter,"[158] and useless and foolish "speculations."[159] Second, in both letters Paul speaks about how the women were susceptible to the false teaching.[160] And third, in 2 Timothy 4:12, Paul notes that he has sent Tychicus to Ephesus. It's altogether possible that "Paul's intent was to have Tychicus relieve Timothy (cf. Titus 3:12)."[161] After all, in this second letter, "Timothy is depicted as reeling from the battle

The Pickoff

and perhaps disheartened by the failure of the corrective measures enjoined in 1 Timothy."[162]

While it's impossible to firmly put dates on each of these letters, we can guess that two to four years have passed between these letters. Unfortunately, Timothy is still dealing with the noises of nonsense, and the continual onslaught has taken its toll on him. Likewise, the noises of nonsense take a toll on many of us.

Paul's advice to Timothy is appropriate for us today. He notes that "endurance" (5x) is critical, as other Christian baserunners have been picked off.[163] In describing how to endure, Paul tells Timothy to:

- "hold on to the example of sound words"[164]
- "protect the treasure" God entrusted to him[165]
- "be strong in the grace that is in Jesus Christ"[166]
- stay focused and compete as to win[167]
- "be diligent" as an approved worker of God[168]
- "flee from youthful lusts and pursue righteousness"[169]
- "continue" in the things he has learned[170]
- "use self-restraint in all things"
- "endure hardship"[171]

With the goal of reaching home safely, these words are applicable to us. We must endure by being strong in grace, staying focused, being diligent, fleeing sin, pursuing righteousness, using self-restraint, and enduring hardship.

In 2 Timothy 2:23, Paul gave Timothy another word of advice that seems particularly relevant to us today. He said, "Refuse foolish and ignorant speculations, knowing that they produce quarrels." Social media, in particular, has constructed a culture that promotes the noises of nonsense. Day after day, we deal with foolish and ignorant arguments that get us nowhere. Such arguments are even enjoyed and applauded. But the great apostle tells us that the noises of nonsense are a threat to Christian baserunners. We must not waste our efforts exploring their foolish conversations. Instead, we must hold fast to the truth we know in Christ.

Philemon—Cultural Voices

Paul opens this letter by saying, "Paul, a prisoner of Jesus Christ." That he mentions his imprisonment often[172] in twenty-five short verses is no coincidence, as he gently confronts Philemon about the awful circumstance of being held in bondage. While Philemon is a "beloved brother and fellow worker,"[173] he is also a slaveholder. Paul writes this letter "as an appeal to accept his runaway slave Onesimus back, no longer as a slave, but rather as a 'beloved brother' (v. 16). A key to Paul's appeal is that Paul and Philemon are partners (v. 17) in the Gospel, as now Onesimus is also."[174]

The unpleasant topic of this letter reminds us of the cultural voices that try to impede our progress on the basepaths. When we support ungodly social mores, we further the work of the enemy. That Christians would even support ungodly standards proves the necessity of coaching Christian baserunners. We live in a world that perverts truth. Going along with that perversion allows darkness into what should be an illuminating light. Considering the topic of slavery in Philemon, it's ironic that adherence to ungodly social mores stunts a person's growth and keeps them in bondage. We must resist the cultural voices that keep us stuck on the basepaths, as acceptance of ungodly truth can potentially lead to a pickoff.

THE WRAP-UP

I read an article online titled, "22 Hilariously Bad Pieces of Advice You Shouldn't Follow."[175] One such piece of advice was sent in from a guy named Joe in California. He said, "As a rookie fireman, I was advised by the older firemen to start smoking. They said it would help acclimate my lungs to the smoke in a building fire." Now that's just classic!

The Pickoff

There are a lot of voices out there, some dispensing good advice and others that seem bent on giving us lung cancer. And maybe thinking of it in those terms is actually helpful, as the voices we listen to can bring life or death.

CHAPTER 6

Imposing One's Will

ANYONE WHO HAS COMPETED in sports can tell you that the mental side of the game is just as important as the physical side. Gifted athletes who ignore the details of the game have a way of letting the team down when it matters most. On the other hand, a steady player with mental toughness is a reliable teammate.

Overall, baseball may not be the best example of "imposing your will" on your opponent. Such language is better suited for high-intensity sports of physicality. Nevertheless, it suits the pitcher vs. baserunner battle well.

While the 2023 season saw MLB implement new rules[176] that limited pickoff attempts per plate appearance, in years past the pitcher could throw over to a base as many times as he wished. While some fans hate when pitchers explore tactic after tactic, I love this cat-and-mouse game and am very unhappy about the rule changes. Watching a pitcher try to impose his will on a runner (e.g., prevent him from stealing) by faking a throw, stepping off, or throwing over a half dozen times is a beautiful battle between the pitcher and runner.

Base burglars always insist on getting a healthy lead off first base. So, in an effort to keep the runner close to the bag, the pitcher will sometimes throw over. Guys with big leads often have difficulty getting back to the bag safely on their feet—they must dive back. If the pitcher can impose his will, the runner will eventually

The Pickoff

get tired of diving back into the base. It's not just the physical fatigue that drains the runner's enthusiasm, it's the mental fatigue. When any type of fatigue sets in, the runner is primed to be picked off. And at the very least, the pitcher will settle for a runner who will simply give up on any attempt to swipe the bag.

THE ENEMY IS RELENTLESS

Having explored Paul's concern for Christian baserunners in the previous chapter, our attention now turns to Peter. In his first letter, Peter writes to the Jewish Christians who are now "scattered," living as "aliens" outside of their homeland.[177] The scattering is the direct result of persecution. In fact, forms of the word "suffer" appear 16x in this short letter, underscoring the seriousness of the situation. As Peter writes to encourage them, he says,

> **12** Beloved, do not be surprised at the fiery ordeal among you, which comes upon you for your testing, as though *something* strange were happening to you; **13** but to the degree that you share the sufferings of Christ, keep on rejoicing, so that at the revelation of His glory you may also rejoice and be overjoyed. **14** If you are insulted for the name of Christ, you are blessed, because the Spirit of glory, and of God, rests upon you (1 Pet 4:12–14).

Peter paints a frightening picture, as he refers to the testing as a "fiery ordeal." Nevertheless, we are blessed, and can even rejoice, when we share in the sufferings of Christ as a "crown of glory"[178] awaits the faithful. Therefore, there is no reason for worry,[179] as our God cares deeply for us.

As Peter proceeds into the conclusion of the letter, he says something similar. He says,

> **8** Be of sober *spirit*, be on the alert. Your adversary, the devil, prowls around like a roaring lion, seeking someone to devour. **9** So resist him, firm in *your* faith, knowing that the same experiences of suffering are being accomplished by your brothers and sisters who are in the world. **10** After you have suffered for a little while, the God of all

grace, who called you to His eternal glory in Christ, will Himself perfect, confirm, strengthen, *and* establish *you* (1 Pet 5:8–10).

Again, Peter presents us with an unpleasant image, this time of a ravenous lion on the prowl. But if God's people will stand firm in the faith, God will perfect his people when he calls them into his eternal glory.

Since we live in an age of nuclear threat, we may not appreciate the terrifying image of a lion. But we should remember, there's a reason the lion has been called the "King of Beasts." So imposing is the lion, that it has as many nicknames as Babe Ruth (e.g., "The Sultan of Swat," "The Bambino," "The Colossus of Clout," etc.). Epithets for the lion include: "The King of the Jungle," "The Lord of the Forest," and even, "The Sultan of the Savanna." Peter could not have chosen a more frightening animal to represent the enemy.

Satan is not merely out to annoy and distract Christ-followers, he wants to "devour" them. As unpleasant as this sounds, the word actually means to "swallow up" ("gulp" down) and "destroy." In other words, the enemy is relentlessly on the prowl looking for whom he may completely consume.

Peter says we must be on the "alert" as the enemy is on the hunt, seeking to impose his will on baserunners who are "suffering" from the fatigue of the Christian race. The foe is persistent in his pursuit of Christian baserunners and will not settle for anyone looking to advance bases. If he must, he will temporarily settle for the Christian who seems unconcerned with advancing on the bases (e.g., advancing in personal growth and advancing kingdom goals). After all, these oblivious baserunners are primed for the eventual pickoff, anyway. It's imperative that we understand that the enemy of God has a single-minded goal, to completely impose his will and pick off all baserunners.

The Pickoff

The Gospels often illustrate the relentlessness of the evil one. Three examples are sufficient in showing how Satan works to impose his will. We may begin with the temptations of Jesus.[180] After Jesus fasted for forty days, the devil came to tempt Jesus on three separate occasions. In each instance, Jesus rebukes the enemy by quoting the truth of God's word. Matthew concludes this section by saying, "Then the devil left him."[181] Luke, however, concludes with the following words—"And *so* when the devil had finished every temptation, he left Him until an opportune time."[182] In other words, the enemy wasn't about to give up. He would do everything within his power to impose his will on Jesus.

A second example is found in Luke 13:10–17. Twice we're told that Satan has bound a woman with a sickness that has lasted for eighteen years. But Jesus comes to her rescue and heals her. Finally, the story of a demon-possessed man in Mark 5:1–20 comes to mind. But this is no "ordinary" possession, we're told that a "legion" of demons was possessing this man's body. While it seems like overkill, a complete waste of demonic power, the story proves how the enemy wishes to completely devour anyone he can.

Each of these (the temptations, eighteen years of illness, and a legion entirely devoted to one person) perfectly illustrates how Satan vigorously attempts to impose his will. He will go to any lengths to accomplish his goal—to keep people away from our Lord so he may destroy them.

SUBMITTING TO THE WILL OF GOD

You can't win a baseball game unless you outscore your opponent. It makes no difference if a team wins by the score of 1–0 or 8–7—you just have to outscore the other team.

I find the Christian life very similar. At times we stumble and give up runs to the opponent. It may even seem as if we're losing now and then. One can imagine the enemy celebrating as we boot a ground ball and mishandle a routine fly ball. And he certainly enjoys watching undisciplined baserunners stumble about.

IMPOSING ONE'S WILL

While Satan attempts to impede Christians from advancing on the basepaths, we must remain firm in the truth of God's word to us. A critical truth we must always remember is found in the big message of Revelation—in the end, the good guys win! Christ, and those who follow him, will forever be victorious.

Saying that someone follows Jesus implies (at least) two things. First, faith must be present in the believer. And second, "following" speaks of action, an action that says something of the believer's submission to the Lord's will. We may think of Jesus calling Peter and Andrew (and then James and John) to follow him.[183] In following after Jesus, we see their faith in action, a demonstration of their submission to the will of God.

Sound baserunning results from attentive runners who have listened to their coaches and have then put into practice those things which were learned. It's pretty simple stuff, and yet it seems as if many MLB games feature a baserunning mistake. For example, it still amazes me that many MLB baserunners fail to pick up their third base coach (i.e., fail to look at the coach) before rounding second base.

Good baserunners are coachable. Likewise, good Christian baserunning is the result of both hearing and doing. When Jesus speaks, we must both listen and obey. Christians are often great at listening, but not always so great at the obeying part. And yet, our obedience, our submission to the Lord's will, is key to our success. Submission guarantees victory, but in our humanness we often resist the very thing that draws us close to our God.

Judas Iscariot, the disciple who betrayed Jesus, is an interesting case study. As we read through John's gospel account of Jesus, we note some alarming issues. First, we know he will eventually betray Jesus.[184] Second, while Judas was appointed as the treasurer of the group, Jesus clearly knows he is also a thief who is pilfering money from the pot.[185] And finally, before the act of betrayal, we learn that "Satan enters him."[186]

Such treachery demands that we ask how in the world Judas could do such a thing. How in the world could Judas remain in

THE PICKOFF

continual contact with Jesus and yet remain unchanged? Clearly, many lessons can be learned, two of which we will note. A first lesson is that lip service is meaningless. Judas called Jesus, "Lord,"[187] but as Jesus says in the Sermon on the Mount,[188] talk is cheap.

A second lesson is that going through the motions offers us no guarantees. If Judas could hang out with Jesus and remain unchanged, then perfect church attendance, in and of itself, certainly means nothing. Talking a good game and hanging out with the right people doesn't mean anything unless a person follows Christ in obedience.

Judas did not allow Christ into his heart. Over and over, Judas heard the words of truth that rolled off the tongue of Jesus. He was among the few who saw miracle after miracle. He was even among the select who spent personal time with the Son of God. And yet, he was not moved to follow the words of Christ. It's through our submission to the will of God, that the Holy Spirit enters into us. But instead, Judas allowed Satan in.

> The fact that the phrase 'entering in' is employed in this connection does not mean so much that Judas was extraordinarily eager to let Satan in as it means that Satan never previously made so determined an attack as now. He realized that he had to exert every effort in this moment of world-crisis to preserve the soul that had almost been touched by the flames of Jesus' love; he knew that he had to try hard to preserve it as a torchbearer of hell.[189]

Judas allowed Satan to impose his will, while all the time Jesus stood next to him and invited him into his marvelous light. As Schilder said,

> How often Jesus had invited, constrained, almost compelled Judas to fall on his knees before Him and to confess everything to this Lord! Repeatedly Jesus used every possible means to recall from the somber depths of the disciple's soul those things which he had suppressed into his unconscious life. If Judas had responded to that invitation, he would thereby have proved that his perverse will had been broken already. Then the Spirit of Christ

would have 'entered into' the soul of Judas triumphantly
... But Judas kept still.[190]

In keeping still, Judas was picked off! And therein lies the problem. When Christ speaks, we must never keep still. We must always respond to the piercing words of Jesus, as his words offer truth. We are amiss if we hesitate to fully embrace his words of life—words that guarantee successful baserunning.

When Jesus says, "Follow Me," like Peter and Andrew, we should immediately follow. But taking first steps with Jesus is simply not enough, even Judas did that. We must keep progressing, as when we hesitate, the enemy takes notice. These moments of hesitation create opportunities for the enemy to get in our ear, get in our mind, and ultimately get in our heart. Satan will say, "Are you sure Jesus is the Son of God? Do you really want to waste your entire life following after some guy who lived 2,000 years ago? The Bible is just a collection of good stories."

If Satan senses our willingness to obey the words of God, he'll just say something like, "Aren't you really busy right now? You can always follow Jesus later. The church isn't going anywhere. If God really loves you, he'll forgive you for putting this off a while."

As we vacillate, Satan schemes and schemes to prevent us from ever reaching first base. After all, a player can't score if they never reach base safely. If by chance someone gets on base, he'll move to "Plan B" and will work to immediately remove them from the bases. But just as our obedience to the words of Jesus enabled us to reach first base, that same obedience will always lead around the bases.

THE ENEMY'S ULTIMATE INABILITY TO IMPOSE HIS WILL

From 1985–1990, Vince Coleman was the most feared baserunner in MLB. The speedy left fielder for the St. Louis Cardinals led the National League in stolen bases in each of these seasons. In fact, Coleman stole over 100 bases in each of his first three seasons with

The Pickoff

the Cardinals (1985-1987) and in these six seasons he amassed an incredible 549 stolen bases, an average of 91.5 per year. To put this into perspective, Ricky Henderson, the all-time stolen base leader, led the American League in stolen bases in five of these seasons,[191] and only totaled 443 during this six-year span.

On June 1, 1986, the Cincinnati Reds hosted the Cardinals, and it was a day to remember for the 26,000 in attendance, as they witnessed a seven minute and twenty-one second sequence that was one for the ages.[192] Lefty Chris Welsh was making his major league debut. As he began the game, he promptly walked Coleman, who then stole both second and third base. Thus, when Coleman singled to start the fifth inning, Welsh was determined to prevent Coleman from repeating his earlier feat.

With one throw after another, Welsh attempted to pick Coleman off first base. After throwing over five times, Cardinals's announcer Jack Buck said, "He's wearing him [Coleman] out over there." In guessing that Coleman was going on the next pitch, the Reds pitched out, only to see Coleman remain at first base.

After thirteen pickoff attempts, Welsh stepped off a couple times causing Buck to say, "He's kept Coleman pinned at first base." In other words, while Welsh was unable to pick off Coleman, he was able to impose his will on him (at least temporarily). Because this game within the game had kept going on and on, after the sixteenth throw to first, Buck said, "I wonder how many times he has thrown over there?"

Welsh would throw over one more time, totaling an incredible seventeen throws to first (also adding several step offs and a pitchout). At this point Buck said, "Coleman is probably so weary, he can't take that first step." But on the very next pitch, after an incredible seven minutes, Coleman swiped second. Speaking of Coleman, Buck said, "Well, he won the battle didn't he."

This incident perfectly illustrates how the enemy tries to impose his will on God's people. He will throw "flaming arrows" (Eph 6:16) as he attempts to eliminate us. If he can't immediately pick us off the Christian path, he'll work vigorously to keep us pinned at first base. Under these conditions, we can't grow in our faith and advance on the basepaths (which primes us for a future pickoff). And he will do everything within his power to simply wear us out, so that we will give up altogether.

But like Coleman, the Christian baserunner has the tenacity and skill set to succeed. In the end, the enemy has no ability to impose his will on God's people. It is our Lord who turns the tables on the enemy, imposing his glorious will in triumph over the enemy. To successfully run the bases, God's people only need to follow the instructions of their coach, the Lord Jesus.

THE WRAP-UP

I love the story of Jesus' transfiguration.[193] Jesus takes Peter, James and John up on a mountain and, before you know it, Elijah and Moses show up. And if that weren't enough, Jesus is also transfigured before them, his face shining like the sun and his clothes turning white as light. But the most awesome part comes when Jesus is speaking with the boys. Matthew 17:5 says, "While he was still speaking, a bright cloud covered them, and a voice from the cloud said, 'This is my Son, whom I love; with him I am well pleased. Listen to him!'"

That short statement really simplifies things—listen to Jesus. While the enemy is out to devour, the Lord looks for followers who will simply listen and obey. Circling the bases could never be so simple.

PART 2
Circling the Bases

CHAPTER 7

Successful Baserunning

THE 1982 WORLD SERIES featured the St. Louis Cardinals and the Milwaukee Brewers. Game 4 included an oddity that you simply don't see every day. With one out in the top of the second inning, Ozzie Smith was on second base and Willie McGee was on third base. Tom Herr came to bat and hit a deep drive to the edge of the warning track in center field.

As Gorman Thomas caught the ball, both Smith and McGee tagged up. McGee began to trot home on the sacrifice fly. However, as Thomas began to plant his back foot so he could throw the ball, he slipped and briefly fell. An alert Smith never stopped and scampered home. So, there you have it, a two-run sacrifice fly by Herr. Now that's successful baserunning!

While the first six chapters detailed the primary methods pitchers use to pick off runners, this chapter focuses solely on successful baserunning. Aspects of what it takes to be an effective baserunner have previously been discussed throughout the book (e.g., making relationship with Christ the number one priority). But here I want to concentrate solely on several baseball metaphors that have clear application for Christian baserunners.

The Pickoff

TAKING PRACTICE SERIOUSLY

Good baserunning doesn't just happen overnight. Like virtually every skill, it takes a commitment to practice. The drills are varied and include things like getting a good secondary lead, taking proper angles as you round the bases, and sliding techniques. The point of application is clear—successful Christian baserunners always work on their relationship with Christ. Likewise, we must always work on building our relationships with others. If you're not, I'd venture to guess that you have too many fractured ones.

Perhaps the easiest way to get the point across is just to say that following Jesus isn't supposed to be a part-time deal. Following Jesus is a full-time way of life that, by default, includes the continual commitment to essential life skills that put a smile on our Lord's face. Commitment to the ways of God is key to the Christian baserunner safely reaching home.

KNOWING THE NUMBER OF OUTS

We've all witnessed baserunners break one of the cardinal rules of baseball—making the first or third out of an inning while trying to take third base. The logic is clear. First, with zero outs a runner should settle for a double (unless they are absolutely sure they can get a triple), as this gives the team two chances to drive him home. Even a ground ball to second base will move the runner to third. This greatly increases the runner's chances of scoring (e.g., sacrifice fly, passed ball).

And second, you should never run yourself into the third out of an inning. Perhaps the most infamous lesson was found in the 1926 World Series. The St. Louis Cardinals were leading the New York Yankees 3–2 in Game 7. Babe Ruth was on first base and decided to try to steal second base (or did he?).[194] He was called out. Not only was the game over, but the World Series was as well. What a dreadful way to lose.

Knowing the number of outs reminds me of how imperative it is to understand the immediate situation. Successful baserunners are not thinking about the previous inning, they are aware of the current moment. This may be likened to the necessity of reading the culture and living in the present.

Not only do Christians often focus on better days past, but they (as observed in local churches) always seem to be running at least a decade behind the current trends. In case you need an example, just think of how long it may have taken your church to move away from hymnals to an overhead projector, and then to a projector mounted on the ceiling (connected to a computer).

Successful baserunners are not thinking about the previous inning, they are aware of the current moment.

Not living in the current moment interferes with alert baserunning. Baserunners must always know how many outs there are. Likewise, Christians must always know the current cultural climate surrounding them.

I probably need to elaborate on why living in the present can help prevent the Christian baserunner from getting thrown out on the bases. It goes back to what I said in chapter 3 about the imperative of being awake and alert. We're not to walk around in life as clueless and mindless drones who contribute nothing to the kingdom. Running the bases in an oblivious fashion makes us prime targets of the opponent.

In 1933, the church in Germany saw a "German Christian" movement growing which mixed church policies with Nazi state goals.[195] The "movement had been founded in 1932 with the aim of creating space for National Socialist ideology within the (Protestant) church."[196] Among its appalling guidelines set forth was the following: "We recognize in race, ethnicity, and nation orders of life given and entrusted to us by God, who has commanded us to preserve them."[197] To top it off, the German Christians were advocating a unified Protestant Reich Church.[198]

The Pickoff

Karl Barth, perhaps the greatest biblical scholar of the twentieth century, would have none of this. In criticizing the movement, Barth said,

> The community of those who belong to the church is not determined by blood or through race, but rather through the Holy Spirit and baptism. If the German Protestant Church were to exclude Christians of Jewish descent or treat them as second-class Christians, then it would have ceased to be a Christian church.[199]

Barth even went as far as writing to Hitler on several occasions.[200] Barth's alertness led Heinrich Scholz to say, "In the hour of the greatest danger you have been the theologian who rescued us from suffocation and led us back to the word."[201] While Barth's outspokenness did not repair all of the damage, he was certainly a light during a very dark time that saw some baserunners being picked off.

We must live in the moment. We must be alert and know the situation that surrounds us. Such attentiveness can prevent us from losing by means of mindless blunders.

KNOWING THE SCORE OF THE GAME

I may be showing my age here, but many aspects of the modern baseball game drive me crazy. Let me set forth a scenario that sadly reflects a very realistic situation we often see today. Let's say your team is batting and is down 2–1 in the ninth inning. The leadoff hitter smokes a double to lead off the inning. The sensible thing[202] to do is to simply hit a ground ball to the right side, to move the runner over to third base. This leaves the team with multiple ways of tying the game.

But we all know what the vast majority of hitters today will do, and it's not the sensible thing. Instead of thinking about how they need to tie the game, they dig in and swing for the fences. And, of course, the most likely outcome here is that the batter simply strikes out. Now the team really needs a hit to tie the game, as all the other possibilities were taken off the table.

Situational thinking is crucial to success. When considering the metaphor, knowing the score of the game is somewhat similar to knowing how many outs there are in an inning. There is, however, a critical difference. Knowing the outs may be likened to thinking about the immediate situation, whereas knowing the score involves big picture processing.

We've all succumbed to the lure of sin. One of the reasons we fail is because we don't consider the big picture ramifications of our actions. A bad decision can snowball into a complexity of problems as its downhill momentum adds layers of consequence. Unfortunately, bad decision after bad decision can sometimes result in depression and in just giving up. These actions, of course, are encouraged by the enemy of God who will use any tactic he can to drive us further from Christ.

Pulling oneself back to big picture processing is especially helpful during such times to restore our faith and reinstall hope. Jesus followers must always remember that the score is stacked in their favor, as Christ has secured the win for his people. Smart baserunners know that, despite the occasional setback, victory awaits them. Remember the score, because as they say, "It's easier to play from ahead than it is from behind." When you're ahead, you play relaxed and confident. And guess what—that's the perfect attitude for a Christ follower. So, know the score.

KNOWING WHO IS COMING UP TO BAT

When I was writing about Babe Ruth getting thrown out at second base to end the 1926 World Series, one of my first thoughts was, "Who was at bat? Could it have been Lou Gehrig?" I mean, how criminal would it be to leave Gehrig at bat? You never want to take the bat out of the hands of a great hitter.

But it wasn't Gehrig. Right-handed hitter Bob Meusel was hitting cleanup,[203] inserted between lefties Ruth and Gehrig. Meusel hit .238 in the World Series with zero RBI. He was no Gehrig.

The Pickoff

If it had been Gehrig, it would have been the perfect example for my upcoming point. In 1997, MLB named Gehrig to their All-Time Team, recognizing him as the best first baseman to ever play the game. And yet there's no doubt in my mind that his greatness has been overshadowed by the Iron Man streak[204] and his "luckiest man on the face of the earth" speech that resulted from his early retirement at age 36. Gehrig, of course, had amyotrophic lateral sclerosis (ALS), a neuromuscular illness that is now often referred to as "Lou Gehrig's disease." Gehrig hit .340 for his career with 493 HR and 1,995 RBI. His career OPS was 1.080, third best behind Ruth (1.164) and Ted Williams (1.116). Just imagine what it was like for the Yankees to boast a lineup with both Ruth and Gehrig.

I'm rambling on about Gehrig as I imagine the hypothetical situation of The Iron Horse standing at the plate while a runner was thrown out to end the World Series. I'm concocting this scenario because I can't think of a more pertinent example. But this imaginary situation will do.

Successful baserunners know who is at bat and who is coming up to bat. You simply don't take unnecessary risks when your best hitters are coming up. In other words, baseball is a team game where players depend on one another to achieve success. The same can be said of the church.

In fact, I find baseball to be the team sport that most closely resembles actual life. Think about it—baseball features a single batter facing a single pitcher. Thus, this team game is often an individual game within the larger context of the team. The Christian life is the same, as we each follow after Christ but also depend on the team (other Christians) to aid in our success. Likewise, we do well to remember how our team depends on us.

On occasion, we may hear someone say something like, "It's just me and Jesus." That is flawed thinking, as God's instructions clearly tell us that it should be "me, Jesus, and his church." We need one another and successful baserunners have a firm grip on this reality.

Yes, it's altogether possible that in an actual baseball game, a runner could score with absolutely no assistance from any of his teammates. For example, he could hit a home run, or he could hypothetically steal second base, third base, and even home (that's just a couple possibilities). But let's get real here for a minute. A player who is only concerned about getting himself home (i.e., selfishly, his stats are more important to him than team success) is less valuable than one who is also conscious of the need to get others around the bases as well. We all know that winning baseball teams feature batters who drive in a lot of runners.

Think about Hank Aaron, who drove in a record 2,297 runs during his career. The Hammer drove himself in 755 times with home runs. That means he drove his teammates in 1,542 times. Now that's teamwork, and that's how we should picture the Christian life. How remarkable would it be if we could each assist in 1,500 Christian baserunners reaching home safely! We must do our part to help Jesus followers reach their destination.

The big point here is that successful baserunners know they don't have to do everything themselves. They allow their teammates to help them achieve success. So, let's remember we need one another to reach our goal.

PAYING ATTENTION TO BOTH THE FIRST AND THIRD BASE COACH

I still remember a staple baserunning drill my coaches used quite often. Everyone on the team lines up over by first base. The first guy pretends he is the baserunner and gets his lead. As the pitcher on the rubber goes into his delivery, the runner takes his secondary lead, and then as he imagines the batter stroking a hit, he takes off for second base. As he begins to round second base, the runner picks up the third base coach who either waves him over to third or stops him at second.

After a while, picking up the third base coach is something that should come quite naturally. That's probably why I'm often astounded at major leaguers who still look over their shoulder at the right fielder. Looking backward over the shoulder slows a runner down and makes him more susceptible to getting thrown out.

The Pickoff

This failure in basic baserunning says one of three things. Either the baserunner never cared enough to run the bases properly, or he wasn't coached well, or he simply doesn't trust his coach.

The lesson here is that good baserunners utilize their coaches. Most often, this results in baserunners "listening" to the first base coach and "watching" the third base coach. The application to following Jesus well is probably rather obvious, as we need to listen to God—we can't afford to commit any of the three blunders listed above.

First, we must care enough about our walk with Christ to pay attention to what he says. Trying to go it alone is a recipe for disaster. This means we must read his word and pray for the Holy Spirit's guidance. Second, we must ensure that we're surrounding ourselves with fellow believers who coach us well. And third, we must put our complete trust in Jesus. Faith in an unseen God can be difficult at times, but our God has shown himself to be completely trustworthy. Whereas an actual baseball coach may occasionally run us into an out, our God will always guide us correctly.

THE WRAP-UP

While the enemy looks to pick Christian baserunners off base, our Lord instructs his people in good baserunning. We must:

- Take practice seriously (work on our relationship with Christ)
- Know how many outs there are (live in the moment, be alert, and know the situation that surrounds us)
- Know the score of the game (remember the big picture—we are victorious in Christ)
- Know who is coming up to bat (let other believers speak into your life)
- Pay attention to the coaches (have faith in a God who is completely trustworthy).

Successful Baserunning

Good baserunning doesn't require great speed or exceptional talent. It simply involves mastering the aforementioned skills.

Love him or hate him, Pete Rose was one of the greatest baserunners we've ever seen. Rose wasn't a "five-tool player" (someone who can hit for average, hit for power, run fast, field exceptionally well, and throw exceptionally well). In fact, Rose was a one-tool player—he could hit. His first scouting report even declared him to be a zero-tool player, saying this about Rose, "Can't run, hit, throw or field. All Rose can do is hustle."[205]

Yet, Rose scored 2,165 runs during his career, the sixth highest total in MLB history. "Charlie Hustle" was an alert and smart baserunner who knew how to win. His achievement remains inspiring, as he reminds us that success can be found by virtually anyone who works hard at the fundamentals.

The news only gets better for Jesus-followers, as success is not found by "virtually anyone" who will follow after Jesus. Instead, victory is found by "all" who will practice good baserunning habits. So, pay attention and run the bases with Christ.

CHAPTER 8

The Necessity of Having Fun

"Some think saying 'Yes' to Jesus is saying 'No' to pleasure and joy and delight and play. This is an insult to everything that is human. Joy is integral to the essence of being human."[206]

—LEONARD SWEET

WILLIE MAYS IS CONSIDERED by many to be the greatest baseball player to ever play the game. His 660 HRs and twelve Gold Gloves speak to his greatness both offensively and defensively. And his Baseball Reference[207] page is so full of accomplishments that one can get lost plowing through all the data. It's probably sufficient to just say, other than pitching, there was nothing Mays couldn't do on a baseball field.

And yet for all his greatness, many fondly remember Mays for the fun he displayed while playing. "He wasn't a polished professional. He was a kid playing baseball. He was out there every day and it looked like he was having the best time of anybody in the ballpark."[208]

Mays "played with joy and abandon. He wanted to win, but also to have fun doing it. To entertain the fans, he wore a hat a little too small for his head so it would fly off as he ran the bases."[209] When Mays was asked if he could have been as successful if he

THE NECESSITY OF HAVING FUN

didn't enjoy it as much, he said, "I don't think that way. How can you not enjoy it?"[210] After all, "playing with joy was all he knew."[211]

Mays once said, "I like to play happy. Baseball is a fun game, and I love it. When the fun leaves, I'll retire."[212] Only Father Time could zap his joy. So, after twenty-three years, at the age of 42, he finally hung up his cleats.

FROM LEGALISTIC CLONES TO JOYFUL HUMAN BEINGS

Beginning a life with Jesus is an exhilarating experience. It's a joy unlike any other. Unfortunately, many church folk attach unbiblical expectations on new converts. Whether it's legalistic rules about church attendance, or an implicit requirement to 'be like us now," these extra biblical expectations are joy zappers.

We may compare the moment to a free agent signing with a new team which has a completely different culture within the front office and clubhouse. There's not only a literal changing of the uniform, but an expected "fall in line" philosophy that can take place.

While not diminishing one's conversion from sinner to saint, nor the process of sanctification, the point here is that new Christians often feel like they should become like everyone else in the church. On one hand, it's only natural, as converts want to change—the evidence of true repentance. And since they don't know what that really means, they look to the people of the church for guidance.

The idea itself is grounded in Scripture, as the Apostle Paul tells Christ-followers to imitate him, as he imitates Christ.[213] We may, however, take the word "imitate" just a bit too far sometimes. Perhaps that's why the NIV translates the text to say, "Follow my example, as I follow the example of Christ."

Paul isn't saying, "Come join my stormtrooper cloning program." In case you're not into *Star Wars*, let me get you up to speed. In *Star Wars II*, we learn that they are literally "clone troopers." Eventually, the clones are replaced by recruits, but nothing really changes. While the stormtroopers initially add an imposing

The Pickoff

dramatical element, they eventually become somewhat comical. Stormtroopers always look the same—they have white clunky uniforms which hinder mobility and fail to prevent mortal wounds from blasters. And they always act the same—not a single one of them can hit the side of a barn when he shoots. Whether they are the originals clones or the later recruits that are made to look and act like clones, they are pretty useless.

No, our Lord isn't looking for useless clones. Instead, he wants to help us become more comfortable in our own skin. God wants us to embrace our uniqueness and use it for his glory. Insightfully, Leonard Sweet says, "The more Jesus fills us, the more we sound like ourselves."[214]

Too often we come to Jesus and think we simply need to fall in line. Not only does that mentality have the stench of legalism all over it, but it's a borefest. And our God is anything but boring! Legalism is the ultimate joy killer that stunts our growth and creativity. But Jesus calls us to the joy of knowing him. It's this joy for the journey that helps us find ourselves.

After all, who are we without God in our lives? Without Christ we feel aimless and unfulfilled, all the time sensing that we're missing out on something in life. That's because a life void of God also leaves an inherent sense of lost identity. God's intent is to bring us close to him, which in turn, brings inner healing.

We often think salvation is the ultimate reward, but the reality is, salvation is the result of the ultimate reward—knowing God. And what we need to grasp is that knowing God also includes finally meeting ourselves. This is because we don't really know ourselves until God is given his proper place. It's only after a person surrenders their life to God that they can learn to become the person God created them to be. It's this coming into oneself that brings fulfillment.

Christian clones aren't very likely to circle the basepaths. There's no joy in just being like someone else and a joyless journey

The Necessity of Having Fun

inevitably comes to an end. When it does, we return to where we started. By contrast, a joyride with Jesus takes place on an endless road of adventure.

A joyless human is hardly human at all. Think about it. God created us to smile, to laugh, and to enjoy life. A life void of such activity is not the human experience God intends for his people. His creation is "good"[215] and a life lived for Jesus should absolutely reflect that truth. Even when life is tough, Paul exclaims that Jesus-followers can rejoice and maintain joy![216]

PLAYING LOOSE

Some players thrive under pressure, and some don't. Success often goes back to the ability to focus, drawing confidence from the countless hours of preparation. But succeeding in the moment can also come down to one critical factor—enjoyment.

People that have fun don't collapse under the pressure of the moment. Instead, they enjoy it. That's not to say that physical mistakes don't happen to everyone now and then. But in the pressure-filled moments that see some tighten up, athletes who are having fun often excel.

We've all witnessed the athlete who allowed the pressure to get to them. In baseball, the strain can be manifested by squeezing the bat too tightly or overthrowing a breaking ball. In essence, when the pressure is on, some people tighten up and try too hard.

Unfortunately, athletes are not alone in feeling the weight of a situation. Life has a way of stressing all of us. Whether it's meeting a deadline at work, finding time to run the kids to every event under the sun, or feeling the heat about an upcoming payment—pressures are everywhere. And where there is pressure, there is anxiety.

God tells us to let the pressure go, as he can shoulder it for us.[217] But, of course, that's easier to say than do. Because anxiety is such a problem for us, the biblical writers repeatedly speak to the topic.

In Jesus' Sermon on the Mount, there is a lengthy section about worry.[218] Jesus paints several scenarios that may cause anxiety, but his message is always the same—do not worry. It's so important to our well-being, that Jesus says it six times. His reasoning is simple, our Father knows[219] all about our concerns. So, why worry?

The Apostle Paul also takes up the topic. He says, "Do not be anxious about anything, but in every situation, by prayer and petition, with thanksgiving, present your requests to God."[220] As crazy as it sounds, he said give thanks when you're worried. In fact, in the previous two verses he even says twice to "rejoice." In other words, we can replace worry with joy, with thanks—while focusing on the fun things in life.

The enemy will try to tell us that everything is not okay. He'll try to turn our attention to the struggle of life, to the alleged impossibility of finding our way out of a difficult situation, and to his accusation that God doesn't care. Indeed, he'll tell us that we should worry. But our Lord tells us that the Father provides for even the smaller, more vulnerable creatures—such as the birds.[221] So, of course, our God will take care of us too.

Worry is a complete waste of energy that is unbefitting to the Christ-follower. We should be clothed in the finest of garments, and burdening ourselves with worry may be compared to a penguin tossing his tuxedo aside, choosing instead to wear an old ripped up hoodie.

Christian baserunners are at their best when they play loose, have fun, and enjoy the game. Sadly, to locate the fun, we sometimes look in life's rearview mirror—to a time in our youth when our life was free from complication.

We can see this loss as teenagers grow into adulthood. College, marriage, children, and working a tedious job to pay bills have a way of bringing out the serious side of a person, causing one to wonder where all the fun in life went.

We see the loss in midlife too. The sadness of being an empty nester, the struggle to lose weight, and the stress of preparing for retirement reminds one of the challenges in life. And if that weren't

The Necessity of Having Fun

enough, the regrets start to set in—the "what ifs," "I could have done more," etc.

And we see the loss in the golden years. What's so golden about living with a failing body—a body that often leads to the loss of one's independence? And experiencing the loss of countless friends and family members leaves one lonely and depressed. The loss can bring a sense that there's nobody left who gets you.

Life is ever-changing, challenging, and arduous. At the same time, another picture must be painted. With adulthood comes the possible joy of marriage, children, and achievement. With middle age, the freedom to travel rejuvenates and grandchildren revive one's strength. And the golden years bring retirement, time to pursue new things, a matured faith, a peak into an unknown future, and even great-grandchildren.

Here's the point. Life is always full of choices. We can let the difficulties of life overcome us, or we can choose the excitement that comes from living. In baseball, the difficulty can be likened to the stress of needing to perform well. Due to the stress of the game, many professional ball players have even retired. When people don't enjoy something, they look to change the situation at hand.

For example, when people don't like what's on television, they start channel surfing. When people don't like the customer service or prices of a restaurant they dine at, they start looking for something to replace it. When people don't enjoy their job, they look for another one. When people don't like their friends, they find new ones. And when people don't enjoy their marriage partner, they even file for divorce.

Lack of enjoyment always precedes change. The same can be said of the church you attend. And we're kidding ourselves if we think people don't give up on Christianity because they feel unsatisfied. If we want to circle the bases, we need to make sure we enjoy the journey.

So how do we go about playing loose in "real life" with Christ? We're all so very different, that I wouldn't dare suggest there is one simple formula for everyone. I can only speak for myself, and so

The Pickoff

I want to relate some keys that have helped me remain steady on the bases.

First, part of my life routine is to inundate myself with music and sitcoms. While Rush is my favorite all-time band and keeps me tapping my fingers to the familiar rhythms that bring me great pleasure, groups like Switchfoot and Whiteheart help keep my mind on godly things. That aside, I listen to a lot of music because it relaxes me. And sitcoms make me laugh, and I like to laugh. I can always tell if I've gone a few days without one or the other.

One of my favorite sitcoms is *Frasier*. In one episode,[222] Frasier takes his girlfriend Claire to Belize. During the first day, everything that can go wrong seems to do so. On the way to the airport, he gets into a fender bender. His flight is then delayed and upon arrival in Belize, he has to ride on a tractor in route to his hotel. Of course, the airline loses his luggage, and to make things worse, the hotel gives his reserved room away (since he arrived late). So, he gets stuck in a room with a poor view. Later, he goes out to dinner only to find out that the restaurant with an ocean view has run out of fish.

After enduring all of this, nobody could really blame Frasier for having a horrible attitude. Claire, however, with exception to the fender bender, has experienced the same disastrous day. But her response is that they should enjoy the restaurant's ocean view. After listening to Frasier complain some more, she reaches her limit and says, "Frasier, we've both had a long day but we're here now. Why can't you just make the most of it?"

And there it is again—life is always full of choices. We can choose to focus on the positive or negative. Focusing on the former helps keep us loose so we can enjoy life.

I can't stress enough how the regularity of music and laughter both help me feel like myself. That's difficult to explain, but I trust you get it. Let me ask, "What makes you feel like yourself? What are the things that give you enjoyment and help keep you centered?"

The Necessity of Having Fun

God knows what activities help make you feel whole, and he wants you to embrace them. There's no need to worry about being a Christian clone—be yourself.

Second, I'm always trying to learn. While I had my master's degree at age thirty-five, I didn't earn my doctorate until I was fifty-three. I'm simply not done learning, and I hope I'll always be able to maintain that attitude. Whatever it is for you, stimulate your mind and allow the Lord to keep pushing you to new places. Resist complacency and enjoy where God takes you.

Third, what is life without the relationships that fill it? We must each make the most of the relationships God has placed in our path. If you want to enjoy life, you can't sit around and wait for people to call you. That mentality is a relationship killer. Take the initiative and call/visit friends and family. What brings joy more than spending time with someone you love?

Finally, a truly enjoyable life comes from walking with God. We should never underestimate how time with God impacts our attitudes and behaviors. If we want to circle the bases, we can only do so with God at our side.

I had previously stated, "to locate the fun, we sometimes look in life's rearview mirror—to a time in our youth when our life was free from complication." I should also add that life was great because we had little responsibility. After all, our parents took care of everything. While adulthood can never take us back to that point, having a relationship with God gets us closer.

We're just flat out wrong if we believe becoming an adult means we enter a phase of life with perpetual, stressful responsibility. While life is often challenging, when we allow God into our lives, he's happy to take on the role of having perpetual responsibility. We do our part, but we hand control over to him. It's the only way you can play loose and have fun.

Let's be honest. Sometimes such talk sounds like "Christianeze," as giving control to God is harder than it sounds. But I don't think it is. On a baseball team (or any other team), we always do our part and relinquish control of everything else over to our teammates and coaches. That's what makes it a team. Each player shares some responsibility for the success of the team. When we translate this to the Christian life, it's even more simplified. We do our part, and God does his part (often using other people to minister to us). With God at the helm, why shouldn't we play loose and stress free?

THE WRAP-UP

It's more than a shame that the word "boring" is often associated with Christianity—it's really a crime against our Creator. Being a Jesus-follower should lead us on the most enjoyable ride of our lives. We must do those things that put us in a position to enjoy the adventure with God, critical things such as spending time with God and experiencing the growth that comes from obedience. Furthermore, we all need to prioritize those things that make us feel alive (e.g., listen to music, laugh, learn).

Living as a Christian clone ends in disaster, as does allowing stress to rule our thoughts. It's when we learn to be our true selves (the discovery of our self in Christ) and turn the troubles of the day over to God, that we can embrace the enjoyment that comes from living. If we want to circle the bases, we should remember what Los Angeles Dodgers star Mookie Betts[223] once said, "Having fun is definitely how you're going to keep yourself loose and be at your best."

PART 3
Extra Innings

CHAPTER 9

The Danger of Standing Still

WITH MIND-BLOWING CONTRACTS GIVEN out to the top sluggers in MLB, it's really no surprise the game has evolved into a "sit back and wait for the long ball" affair. After all, if players don't get big contracts for running the bases well, making consistent contact, or for sacrificing themselves for the team (e.g., moving runners from second to third), then fewer players will arrive on the major league scene with these skill sets. The unfortunate result is a lack of action on the basepaths (e.g., stealing, hit-and-runs, sacrifice bunts).

Thus, the modern game has evolved into what was formerly called "American League Baseball," a brand of baseball where a player gets to first base and simply stands there until someone hopefully drives him in with a home run. This absence of action is not only boring to watch, but it serves as yet another lesson for Christian baserunners.

PLAN B

The enemy's primary plan of action is to pick off Christian baserunners. But if he's unable to accomplish his immediate goal, he'll settle for baserunners who just stand around and do virtually nothing to impact the result of the game.

Baserunners who stand around and wait for the home run ball aren't very engaged. Think about it. They don't bother taking

The Pickoff

aggressive leads because they don't plan on going anywhere, anyway. They really have little reason to worry about any signs coming from the third base coach because the basic plan is to simply stand there and wait for the long ball. Therefore, it's highly unlikely they'll ever see a "hit-and-run" sign, a sacrifice bunt sign (so they can be moved into scoring position), or a steal sign.

Having Christian baserunners unengaged is a nice Plan B for the enemy. After all, an unengaged runner isn't really concerned about much going on around him. And better yet, unengaged runners get bored and can somewhat "check out." We may think of the person who becomes a Christian and then stands around waiting for heaven. Surely, Satan approves of us standing still, as inactivity is simply not a godly activity.

In John Stott's classic book on the Sermon on the Mount, he summarizes Jesus' words[224] about the necessity of "acting" on his words (versus only hearing) by saying:

> The truth on which Jesus is insisting in these final two paragraphs of the Sermon is that neither an intellectual knowledge of him nor a verbal profession, though both are essential in themselves, can ever be a substitute for obedience. The question is not whether we *say* nice, polite, orthodox, enthusiastic things to or about Jesus; nor whether we *hear* his words, listening, studying, pondering and memorizing until our minds are stuffed with his teaching; but whether we *do* what we say and *do* what we know, in other words, whether the lordship of Jesus which we profess is one of our life's major realities.[225]

Christian baserunning cannot be equated with standing still.

Christian baserunning cannot be equated with standing still. Of course, if the enemy can't pick us off base, he'll try to convince us that making Jesus our Savior is enough activity for a lifetime. But nothing could be further from the truth. Submission to the lordship of Jesus is demonstrated by life activity. And one thing is for sure—obedience to Jesus is a life of interesting, challenging, and even uneasy movement.

While the enemy will adjust his plan from pickoff to inactivity, Jesus tells Christian baserunners to immediately start looking for signs coming from the third base coach (the Holy Spirit). Being an attentive baserunner shows we understand we will soon be on the move.

Jesus tells us to "follow" him. Likewise, Paul tells us to "walk"[226] in him. These verbs speak volumes. Technically, "standing" is also a verb when we say, "Someone is standing at first base." By the same token, we could say someone is "sitting" at first base to also show how a verb functions in a sentence. But since we describe verbs as action words, both "standing" and "sitting" are dreadful examples of showing action.

Jesus would never instruct us to go stand at first base and wait for the hopeful big moment that will drive us in. He wants to push us into action so we can make a difference in the world. As Leonard Sweet said, "Jesus didn't die on the cross and rise from the dead so we could sit around and do nothing."[227]

We must confess, Plan B is rather brilliant. "Accept Jesus (trot or even walk to first base) and then just stand there until either Jesus returns or you die." The enemy can theologically spin that to lure us into a false sense of meaning and security. But Jesus teaches us that belief and confession are only the beginning of the journey.

A journey should lead somewhere—and we don't wait until death to continue the trip. Consider how you gas up your vehicle before taking a road trip. It's ready to travel, but to simply sit at the gas station would rob you of the adventure awaiting. So, you turn the key and get moving. Coming to Jesus is similar in that he essentially fills our gas tank and beckons us to head out on the road.

It's those who do the "will of the Father" that truly know Jesus.[228] Jesus didn't come just to save souls; he came to save body, mind, and spirit.[229] This is why standing around and merely waiting for heaven is a gross misunderstanding of what it means to be a Jesus follower.

The Pickoff

Reflecting on how some runners arrive at first base with no intention of ever going anywhere provides another lesson. Some pitchers will willingly pitch around dangerous hitters. In fact, if they have too, they'll happily walk a hitter so they can aggressively go after the guy they want to attack. Having said this, they're much less willing to put aggressive runners on base.

Pitchers aren't exactly squeamish with a non-aggressive runner standing at first, as he often becomes victim of the old twin-killing[230] anyway. But a walk can quickly turn into a double if the guy steals second base, and when runners get moved into scoring position everything changes. In fact, when this happens the pitcher's attention becomes a bit more divided between the hitter and runner—and that can lead to trouble.

The point is that the enemy is never happy with a Christian baserunner who poses a threat on the basepaths, that's exactly why the pickoff is always on his mind. But if the enemy sees a rather disinterested and inert baserunner, he'll reinforce the idea that safely standing at first base is good enough. It's as if he says, "It's great to be aboard the good ole gospel ship. Just live in the glow of Christ and remember that he wants to bless you—so stand there and hoard the blessings. There's no reason to go anywhere."

OFF AND RUNNING

Joe DiMaggio's record 56-game hitting streak (May 15–July 16, 1941) is one of the most remarkable records in sports. Another way of expressing the streak is to say that he hit "safely" in fifty-six consecutive games. With umpires calling runners both "safe" and "out," we understand the terminology well.

The idea of "safety" conjures up the thought that some are happy to anchor themselves to first base, as venturing off the base is dangerous. One may say, "Why mess with a good thing?" And as previously stated, the enemy will support our feeling of safety—as long as that feeling is coupled with immobility. It's noteworthy that DiMaggio also scored 56 runs during the 56-game hitting streak, as he was not content to stand around inattentively.

The Danger of Standing Still

The irony is that safely standing still is an illusion, as complacency is in complete contrast to "following" after Jesus. We may think of the disciples of Jesus who were told to "go" and make disciples.[231] Or perhaps Paul's praise for the Christians at Colossae comes to mind, as he acknowledges how their lives have been bearing fruit.[232] Or maybe you recall the Christians at Philippi who generously joined in Paul's ministry by financially supporting him.[233] The New Testament is full of these "moving" examples.

A Jesus-follower must run the bases, as there is no other way to serve Christ. Arriving at first base is not enough as the goal is to make it home. Therefore, when we arrive at first, we must read the signs from the third base coach and eventually get off and running.

THE WRAP-UP

It's been about twenty-five years ago now, but I still remember what Dr. Wayne Shaw (longtime preaching professor at Lincoln Christian Seminary in Illinois) said one day in class. I don't recall the lecture, the primary topic at hand, or anything else but I remember one singular statement. It was this—"Finish Well."

I've kept these words close to my heart. When I consider his challenging words of encouragement, it's difficult to imagine just standing at first base, happy that I arrived safely to the first of four targeted destinations. After all, as a player you must always have your eyes on the next base.

In baseball the runner may benefit from a home run and find himself just slowly trotting around the bases. But standing and waiting to trot is surely not imagery befitting a Jesus-follower. We must finish well, and to finish well we must put ourselves in motion for Jesus.

CHAPTER 10

Not a Game

YOU DON'T WRITE A book like this unless you love the game of baseball. But we must remember that living for Jesus is no game. In fact, Jesus repeatedly tells us that our decision to follow him, or not follow him, results in either life or death. The latter is a reality we often choose not to think about, as many leave this world without ever coming to Christ. Furthermore, we certainly tire of hearing of an enemy who would love to destroy us. Nevertheless, we must not forget these truths.

I must say, I was reluctant to change metaphors at this point in the book. After all, you didn't sign up for this when you started this "baseball" book. And, of course, war is much more gruesome than some guy getting picked off base. But I think that's the point. War is gruesome, it's ugly, and people perish along the way.

So, to drive home the gravity of the situation, I added this chapter. In Part 1 of the book ("Erased on the Bases"), each of the first six chapters explained how baserunners can become victims to the pickoff artist. Here, I provide true war stories that parallel the driving thought of those chapters. The parallel is fitting, as the Apostle Paul sometimes referred to Jesus-followers as "soldiers."[234] Paul knew we were at war, and thus the war imagery is important to grasp.

By the way, in no way will I depict any army or country as righteous or unrighteous in their war efforts. The illustrations are simply presented as real-life examples that drive home the seriousness of the war tactics. And whether we like it or not, we are at war with spiritual forces.

THE ART OF DECEPTION (CHAPTER 1)

Operation Mincemeat

One of the craziest stories of wartime deception occurred during World War II in 1943. British agents created the ruse that Nazi intelligence fell for hook, line and sinker. Operation Mincemeat[235] "involved planting forged documents upon a dead body before setting him adrift in neutral Spanish waters, with the aim of the papers ending up in German hands."[236] British intelligence hatched this elaborate scheme "to convince the Germans that the Allied forces were planning to invade Greece rather than Sicily."[237]

The "drowned" man was actually a Welsh tramp (Glyndwr Michael) "whose body was obtained in a London morgue by British intelligence officers Charles Cholmondeley and Ewen Montagu, the brains behind Operation Mincemeat."[238] Then, they "transformed" Michael into Major William Martin of Britain's Royal Marines by creating a false identity. The British agents even went as far as giving William Martin a complete backstory that included "a fiancée waiting for him at home."[239]

"The false intelligence found its way onto Hitler's desk and was evidently believed as Germany ordered tank divisions, artillery and boats to defend Greece, Sardinia and the Balkans. When Allied troops invaded Sicily on 10 July 1943, the Nazis were caught unawares."[240] The deception "helped further Italian leader Benito Mussolini's downfall and turn the tide of the war towards an Allied victory in Europe."[241]

When opponents are at war, they'll do virtually anything to obtain victory. As illustrated by Operation Mincemeat, deceptive tactics involve creativity. It's no wonder the enemy of God is always inventing new schemes as he attempts to pick off God's people. In

The Pickoff

the end, Satan will lose the war, but we must face up to the fact that he manages to win many battles as he wages war against God.

Our job is simple—we are to run the bases safely, and to help our fellow teammates do the same. To do so, we must be keenly aware of the fact that a real enemy would love to deceive us and pick us off base. Like a great pickoff artist who straddles the line of what is legal or illegal, Satan works to deceive and confuse his opponents. But our Lord tells how to recognize deception and charts a safe path for us that rests in his truth.

QUICK FEET (CHAPTER 2)

The Battle of the Little Bighorn

One of the most well-known battles in US history is the Battle of the Little Bighorn. The battle took place on June 25, 1876, near the Little Bighorn River in the Crow Indian Reservation in southeastern Montana Territory.[242] The tensions between the US and the Lakota Sioux, Cheyenne, and Arapaho Indians began with the discovery of gold on parts of Native American lands.[243]

Things escalated[244] on January 31st, when Sitting Bull and his followers ignored the US Government's deadline to relocate to reservations. The next day, the issue was turned over to the War Department, and on February 8, Generals Terry and Crook were notified that the War Department had "ordered operations against hostile Indians."[245]

On June 22, Lieutenant Colonel George Armstrong Custer and twelve companies of the 7th Cavalry were "ordered to march up Rosebud Creek in pursuit of Sitting Bull."[246] At dawn on June 25, Custer led his men to the Little Bighorn Valley. By the end of the day, "Custer and some 200 men in his battalion were attacked by as many as 3,000 Native Americans; within an hour, Custer and all of his soldiers were dead."[247] Thus, it's commonly referred to as "Custer's Last Stand." The battle "marked the most decisive Native American victory and the worst U.S. Army defeat in the long Plains Indian War."[248]

Not a Game

Custer's failure was the result of inaccurate assessment, as he underestimated the number of Indians who were fighting under the command of Sitting Bull. Custer estimated the number of opposition fighters would be about 800, as he had no idea that thousands of "reservation Indians" had joined Sitting Bull's ranks for the summer buffalo hunt.[249]

Likewise, Christians often underestimate the enemy. Even worse, they sometimes act as if there is no enemy. Such mindsets can prove disastrous to Christian baserunners, as the enemy is out to "steal, kill, and destroy."[250] Successful baserunners must always remember one clear truth—there is an enemy who wishes to pick us off base.

We're involved in a spiritual war with unseen forces. Thus, accurate assessment of a situation is always crucial and must be followed with quick action that results in safety.

CAUGHT SLEEPING (CHAPTER 3)

The Battle of Trenton

Perhaps the most famous painting depicting the American Revolution is *Washington Crossing the Delaware*, a painting by Emanuel Leutze. The artwork captures the iconic event that led to Revolutionary General George Washington (the Commander-in-Chief of the Continental Army) commanding the battles at Trenton and Princeton, New Jersey, in 1776–77. Washington's victories against Hessian and British forces spanned nine days (December 26–January 03) and "restored American morale and renewed confidence in Washington."[251]

On Christmas night, Washington led a detachment of 2,400 troops from their encampment in Pennsylvania across the treacherous icy Delaware River and then marched nine to ten miles south to Trenton, New Jersey, "where about 1,400 Hessians, fighting in service to Great Britain, were garrisoned."[252] Washington's troops navigated their way across the Delaware in columns that stretched a mile long.[253]

The Pickoff

One column, under Maj. Gen. John Sullivan, would approach Trenton from the west, while the second, under Maj. Gen. Nathanael Greene, would attack from the north. They began their march south about 4:00 am, navigating the predawn darkness and blinding snow. Washington's two columns arrived on the outskirts of Trenton about 8:00 AM, and their audacious attack took the garrison completely by surprise.[254]

Washington caught the Hessians off guard because he had recruited a spy who helped convince the German soldiers that no attack was looming. Because they let their guard down, "the colonial forces were able to parlay an element of surprise into a resounding victory on the morning of December 26."[255]

In the end, the Americans captured 900 prisoners and a payload of guns and ammunition. More than twenty Hessians were killed, with eighty being wounded. Astonishingly, although five Americans were wounded, no Americans were killed.[256]

The Hessian defeat at Trenton is a reminder to soldiers in battle that they should always be on the alert. The enemy is relentless and is actively working to defeat God's people, and like Washington, he'll take a victory at the hands of those who simply let their guards down. Successful baserunners remain awake and alert. They remain steadfast in prayer, build relationship with Christ, and rely on the guidance of the Holy Spirit.

CAUGHT LEANING (CHAPTER 4)

The Battle of Gettysburg

The Battle of Gettysburg was the bloodiest battle of the American Civil War. During the three days of combat (July 1–3, 1863) there were 50,000 casualties. Gettysburg was the turning point in the Civil War, as Confederate General Robert E. Lee's attempt to invade the North was turned back by Union soldiers, essentially ending the Confederacy's hopes of creating an independent nation.

NOT A GAME

Having defeated the Union army at Chancellorsville, Virginia, in May, Lee's forces were confident as they began their second invasion of the North at Gettysburg, Pennsylvania. Lee's aggression at Gettysburg, however, serves to remind us that moving too hastily can have dire consequences.

"On July 1, the advancing Confederates clashed with the Union's Army of the Potomac, commanded by General George G. Meade, at the crossroads town of Gettysburg."[257] The next day, "the Union Army had established strong positions from Culp's Hill to Cemetery Ridge. Lee assessed his enemy's positions and determined—against the advice of his defensively minded second-in-command, James Longstreet—to attack the Federals where they stood."[258]

Previous confederate successes had convinced Longstreet "that the war could be won by adopting a tactical defensive posture while conducting strategic offensive operations."[259] His belief was that Cemetery Ridge "was too strong to be stormed successfully."[260] Thus, Longstreet "advised Lee to move around the federal right flank, forcing Meade out of position & onto ground more favorable for the Army of Northern Virginia."[261]

Lee disregarded Longstreet's advice, not once, but twice, for on July 3, Lee ordered General George Pickett's assault on Cemetery Ridge. Despite Longstreet's protests, Lee ordered fewer than 15,000 troops to march "some three-quarters of a mile across open fields to attack dug-in Union infantry positions."[262] "Pickett's Charge" ended in disaster, as "Union infantry opened fire on the advancing rebels from behind stone walls while regiments from Vermont, New York and Ohio hit both of the enemy's flanks. Caught from all sides, barely half of the Confederates survived, and Pickett's division lost two-thirds of its men."[263] In the end, Lee's massive assaults "nearly broke federal lines on the 2nd, but ended in a magnificent failure on the 3rd."[264]

While some believe Lee was simply determined to attack, it's also been said that "Lee decided on Gettysburg, not out of an uncontrollable emotional zeal, but because it was the safest and best choice given the circumstances he faced."[265] In truth, "Lee knew

THE PICKOFF

very little about the enemy's location and strength. He knew only that two of the seven Union corps were in front of him, leaving five unaccounted for at that point."[266] Consequently, "Lee made the decision he did based on what he thought was best at the moment."[267]

Lee's decision-making demonstrates how moving without perfect guidance can result in ruin. Not only did Lee fail to heed the advice of someone who apparently knew better, but he moved with incomplete information. He did what "he thought was best," a problem we have all repeated time and time again when we fail to consult with God.

While it's one of the most difficult lessons to learn, our self-reliant nature will often fail us. We must always remember—Christian baserunners are assured to move safely around the bases when they seek the will of God. "Guessing and going," a poor attempt to steal strategy, often proves disastrous. And running the bases without the blessing of God is like the road signs that say, "Travel at your own risk."

BAD ADVICE (CHAPTER 5)

Operation Overlord (D-day)

As Adolph Hitler's Nazi Germany was taking over Europe in 1943, the Allies created an offensive that was so complex, it took nearly a year to plan the elaborate deception, code-named Operation Bodyguard. [268] At the center of this massive invasion "that would liberate the continent and turn the tide of World War II"[269] was Operation Overlord (D-day).

On June 6, 1944, the US Navy began Operation Overlord and landed approximately 156,000 Allied soldiers on the Normandy beaches in northern France. Within just a "few days about 326,000 troops, more than 50,000 vehicles and some 100,000 tons of equipment had landed. By August 1944, all of northern France had been liberated, and in spring of 1945 the Allies had defeated the Germans. Historians often refer to D-Day as the beginning of the end of World War II."[270]

NOT A GAME

Hitler knew the Allies were going to invade Europe, but he didn't know where the assault would take place—and he wouldn't know until it was too late. Operation Overlord was so multifaceted, it's been called "perhaps the greatest and most successful use of deliberate deception in 20th-century warfare."[271]

At the heart of the operation was a web of faulty information[272] the Allies kept feeding the Germans. For instance, the Allies flipped more than a dozen German spies to their cause, ultimately using them to feed faulty information to Berlin.[273]

The Allies would also broadcast "endless hours of fictitious radio transmissions"[274] to deceive the Nazis. These broadcasts included troop and supply movements, talk about cold weather issues (e.g., ski bindings) that caused Hitler to deploy troops to Scandinavia just weeks before D-day,[275] and fake wedding notices for fake soldiers. Allied General Dwight Eisenhower even "fed that delusion with false radio traffic."[276]

The misinformation continued even after the successful D-day landing. "Three days later, Spanish businessman Juan Pujol Garcia, who was one of Britain's most valuable double agents, fed information to Berlin that the Normandy landing was merely a 'red herring' and that the most critical attack was yet to come with the First Army poised to strike at Pas de Calais."[277] Garcia even "pointed out that Patton had yet to move from England. So trusted was Garcia that Hitler delayed releasing reinforcements from Pas de Calais to Normandy for seven weeks after D-Day as the Allies gained the toehold they needed to achieve victory in Europe."[278]

Operation Overlord serves as a powerful example of what can happen when we listen to the wrong voices as Hitler did. The enemy of God joyfully uses misinformation in his attempt to pick off Christian baserunners. The fact that we are bombarded with wrong voices (e.g., worldly wisdom, legalism, agitators, hatred, nonsense), means we must be able to distinguish God's voice above all others. As we recognize and follow his voice of truth, we will find safety.

The Pickoff

IMPOSING ONE'S WILL (CHAPTER 6)

Operation Desert Storm

On August 2, 1990, Iraq's president Saddam Hussein ordered the invasion of Kuwait. Despite Iraq boasting the fourth largest army in the world, due to the swift action of the United Nations Security Council and "a massive U.S. led air offensive known as Operation Desert Storm,"[279] the liberation of Kuwait came as early as February 28, 1991.

Iraq's defeat was the result of forty-two days (Jan 17–Feb 28) of unrelenting attacks forged by a cooperative effort of NATO allies. "The coalition effort benefited from the latest military technology, including Stealth bombers, Cruise missiles, so-called 'Smart' bombs with laser-guidance systems and infrared night-bombing equipment. The Iraqi air force was either destroyed early on or opted out of combat under the relentless attack."[280]

To say that the attacks were relentless almost seems like an understatement, as it's been reported that "on many days there were over 2500 . . . missions."[281] In fact, the "coalition attacked more targets in Desert Storm's first day than the entire Eighth Air Force hit in Europe over the course of two years in World War II."[282] Furthermore, "never before in history had as many separate targets been attacked in less time than in Desert Storm. The results were to paralyze, confuse, and ultimately defeat Saddam Hussein's gambit into Kuwait."[283]

Relentlessness is often a sound tactic, and sometimes the strategy of a desperate opponent. In Satan's case, it's the latter. He understands what Christ accomplished for God's people, and yet he works relentlessly to pick Christian runners off base. Operation Desert Storm should serve as a stern reminder to us that an enemy looks to bombard us with challenge after challenge that will eventually wear down our will to follow after God. But praise be to God, if we submit to the will of our Lord, the enemy is unable to impose his will in our lives.

Not a Game

THE WRAP-UP

Stories of war are always unpleasant. Likewise, I've yet to meet anyone who gets excited when reading biblical accounts that involve hell and/or demonic forces. The ideas are so uncomfortable that we often choose to block out such notions from our mind. We all know, however, that burying our heads in the sand will only make things worse.

In war, people die in battle. Unfortunately, the same is true in spiritual war. Thus, it's imperative that God's people recognize and avoid battle tactics that can lead to their demise. Moreover, soldiers for Christ must heed the voice of the commander, for our Lord knows the way to victory.

Conclusion

CLAYTON KERSHAW HAS BEEN one of the most dominant pitchers of this century. In Kershaw's first seventeen years (2008–2024) with the Los Angeles Dodgers, the lefty has collected three Cy Young awards as the National League's best pitcher (and was twice the runner-up). His career statistics are simply mind-boggling, as he has posted 79.4 WAR and a microscopic 2.50 ERA.[284] To put his dominance into perspective, the vast majority of starting pitchers in MLB will never post a single season ERA under 3.00.

Due to Kershaw's absolute dominance of major league hitters, his great pickoff move may be overlooked by the average fan. Watching Kershaw pick off a runner often leaves me in shock, as I can honestly say that I've never seen a pitcher make it look so easy. While he can be very deceptive, he also features a variety of pickoff moves.

Kershaw's arsenal is reminiscent of the enemy of God who explores tactic after tactic in his pursuit of picking off baserunners. But while the Bible paints the devil as the relentless opponent of God, we must always remember that he is absolutely powerless against those who stand firm in Christ.

In John 10,[285] Jesus tells us that he is the Good Shepherd. It's a passage to enjoy over and over, as it's one of the most comforting passages in the entire New Testament. Jesus tells us that he is the door for the sheep. Then he says, "If anyone enters through Me, he will be saved, and will go in and out and find pasture. The thief comes only to steal and kill and destroy; I came so that they would have life, and have *it* abundantly."

The Pickoff

While Jesus calls false teachers "thieves and robbers" in verse 8, it's highly likely that Jesus has Satan in mind in verse 10, as there are contrasts between "Jesus"/"thief" and "life"/"destroy." Satan looks to rob (to pick off sheep), but Jesus is a door of safety.

Jesus continues in speaking of how "the good shepherd lays down his life for the sheep." Yet, he clarifies that, although he will sacrifice his life, he will ultimately "take it back." He tells how the Father loves him, and how God is his Father. It's at this point the Jews say that Jesus has a demon and is completely insane. Jesus responds by saying,

> "I told you, and you do not believe; the works that I do in My Father's name, these testify of Me. But you do not believe, because you are not of My sheep. My sheep listen to My voice, and I know them, and they follow Me; and I give them eternal life, and they will never perish; and no one will snatch them out of My hand. My Father, who has given *them* to Me, is greater than all; and no one is able to snatch *them* out of the Father's hand. I and the Father are one (John 10:25–30).

The word "snatch" is used in both verses 28 and 29. It speaks of how one may attempt to forcefully, or even suddenly, take someone.[286] The image of a "sudden" snatching brings to mind the pickoff. The enemy is a thief who will attempt to get what he wants by force or by surprise—it makes no difference to him how he may succeed in his mission to devour God's people. But Jesus is adamant in that "no one" is able to snatch his sheep away.

Jesus is clear in his simple instructions for safe baserunning. Again, he said, "My sheep listen to My voice, and I know them, and they follow Me."[287] As mentioned previously, we must "listen" and "follow." The action of following speaks to our obedience. Good listening is not displayed in our ability to win Bible trivia contests. Good listening is defined by actionable follow-up. As James said, we must be doers of the word, and not mere hearers.[288]

Baserunners who only listen are like vulnerable sheep who have drifted away from the shepherd, becoming prey to wolves who are looking to "snatch" them away.[289] But baserunners who

Conclusion

both listen and "follow" the shepherd need not worry. The wolf is not greater than the shepherd who tends the flock. Likewise, Satan is no match for our Lord Jesus. Satan may be a master pickoff artist, and he can throw over all day long—but he'll never pick off the Christian who both listens and obeys.

ENDNOTES

CHAPTER 1

1. Baseball Reference lists the seven pitchers with a minimum of seventy-five pickoffs. All seven are left-handed: Steve Carlton (146), Mark Buehrle (100), Andy Pettitte (98), Jerry Koosman (82), Kenny Rogers (79), Mark Langston (78), and Warren Spahn (75). Baseball-Reference.com, "Pitching Season & Career Finder."

2. The following may also be of interest. Rule 8.05(a) says that it's a balk when, "The pitcher, while touching his plate (the rubber), makes any motion naturally associated with his pitch and fails to make such delivery." Additional comment says, "If a left-handed or right-handed pitcher *swings his free foot past the back edge of the pitcher's rubber*, he is required to pitch to the batter except to throw to second base on a pick-off-play." While the comment mentions right-handed pitchers, the illegal pickoff move to first base (involving the free foot swinging past the back edge of the rubber) can only be accomplished by left-handed pitchers. While this is not the primary means of deception pickoff artists employ, it's something within their ability.

3. To avoid such embarrassment, runners are taught to run only after they locate the ball.

4. The Bible also says Satan is a "liar." In describing the devil in John 8:44, Jesus says, "he is a liar and the father of lies." We're also told Satan is a "tempter" and "accuser," terms that also speak to him being a liar. After all, Satan tempts us to do things by portraying them as less harmful than they are. Furthermore, his accusations are based on lies.

5. Matthew 7:15.

6. John 14:6.

7. Luke 8:4–15.

8. 2 Timothy 4:3–4.

9. Ephesians 4:14.

10. James 1:22.

11. Hebrews 12:1.

12. John 10:27.

13. Ephesians 5:23–25.

14. Proof-texting is essentially taking a text and making it mean whatever you want. For example, Philippians 4:13 says, "I can do all things through Him who strengthens me." A person could take that verse and say something

Endnotes

like, "All things, means all things" while never considering the overall context where Paul speaks of learning to be content in various circumstances.

15. McNeal, *Missional Renaissance*.

16. Sweet, *I Am a Follower*.

17. Womble, *Beyond Reasonable Doubt*.

18. The Sermon on the Mount is found in Matthew 5–7.

19. Matthew 5:14.

20. Matthew 5:16.

21. Matthew 5:16.

22. James 2:17.

23. 1 Timothy 5:8.

24. Matthew 5:44.

25. King Jr., "Love of Enemy," 142.

26. Womble. This is from a book I'm working on that I hope to call *The Red Zone* (Devotion 17).

27. Romans 5:10.

28. Matthew 7:7.

29. Matthew 7:11.

30. See 1 Timothy 3:1–13 as an example.

31. Romans 6:1–2.

CHAPTER 2

32. Shields had 38 career pickoffs.

33. Kepner, "Pickoff Tips from James Shields."

34. Each base has an immediate dirt area "cut out" in the grass. This enables runners to slide on dirt.

35. Kepner, "Pickoff Tips from James Shields."

36. Bernier, "Base Running 4."

37. When athletes suddenly lose their ability to perform routine skills, their sudden hiccup is referred to as the yips. Former second baseman Steve Sax encountered the yips when he suddenly had trouble making throws to first base. Numerous pitchers, such as Steve Blass and Rick Ankiel, have also seen their careers ruins by the yips. Golfers sometimes display the yips when they suddenly can't sink simple short putts.

ENDNOTES

38. Muskat, "Lester Tested, Foils Strategy with Rare Pickoff."

39. 2 Corinthians 4:4.

40. 2 Corinthians 2:11.

41. Ephesians 6:13.

42. Ephesians 6:13.

43. This paragraph references various texts in Romans 6.

44. Judges 13–16.

45. Delilah attempts to discover the secret to Samson's strength, and he simply toys with her. The first time is when he says, "If anyone ties me with seven fresh bowstrings that have not been dried, I'll become as weak as any other man" (Judg 16:7). The second is, "If anyone ties me securely with new ropes that have never been used, I'll become as weak as any other man" (Judg 16:11). The last one is, "If you weave the seven braids of my head into the fabric on the loom and tighten it with the pin, I'll become as weak as any other man" (Judg 16:13).

46. Matthew 5:29

CHAPTER 3

47. Muder, "Bench's Excellence."

48. Baseball Reference, "Johnny Bench."

49. Arndt, Gingrich, Danker, & Bauer, *Greek-English Lexicon of the New Testament*, 167.

50. Arndt, Gingrich, Danker, & Bauer, *Greek-English Lexicon of the New Testament*, 14.

51. For example, Ephesians 6:18.

52. Acts 20:28–31; 1 Corinthians 16:13; Ephesians 6:18; Colossians 4:2; 1 Thessalonians 5:1–11; 1 Peter 5:8.

53. 1 Peter 5:8.

54. Acts 20:28–31.

55. Acts 20:25, 38.

56. Acts 20:36.

57. Colossians 4:2.

58. Ephesians 6:19–20 and Colossians 4:3–4.

59. 1 Thessalonians 5:7–8.

ENDNOTES

60. Arndt, Gingrich, Danker, & Bauer, *Greek-English Lexicon of the New Testament*, 538.

61. Ephesians 6:17 and 1 Thessalonians 5:8.

62. MLB, "Willians Astudillo Picks Off Shane Robinson."

63. John 14:6.

64. John 10:7, 9.

65. Acts 1:1–11.

66. John 17:11–12, 15, 21, 23–24.

67. John 13:2, 27; 17:12; Luke 22:3.

68. John 17:11, 21–23.

69. John 17:17, 19.

70. John 14:6.

71. John 17:13.

72. John 17:26.

73. Hebrews 12:2.

74. Sweet, *Aqua Church 2.0*.

CHAPTER 4

75. Dickey won the N. L. Cy Young Award in 2012 while pitching with the New York Mets.

76. MLB, "SD@TOR."

77. Murphy, *Proverbs*, 20–21.

78. Koptak, *Proverbs*, 120.

79. Joshua 1:1–5.

80. Joshua 9:1–2.

81. Joshua 9:3–15.

82. Joshua 9:7.

83. Joshua 9:17. All of these sites fall within the territory of Benjamin. Hess, *Joshua*, 200.

84. 2 Samuel 21:1–6.

85. James 2:19.

86. James 1:22.

ENDNOTES

87. Hebrews 12:1.

88. Hebrews 11:1.

89. Romans 4:11, 16.

90. Hebrews 11:39–40.

91. Sweet, *Jesus Human*, 301. Len also provides insight about the biblical image of the mandorla. He notes the presence of bud-blossom-fruit and says, "God cares, not just about the fruits. God cares about the buds and blossoms too. God cares about the bud that you can see now but that you may never see come to fruition in your lifetime. God cares about the buds that have moved to blossoms, but may never come to fruition in your lifetime" (300). He adds, "God knows us by our buds and blossoms, not just our fruits. Jesus' whole ministry was not about just 'fruits' but about buds and blossoms. He was planting buds and blossoms that would not come to fruition in his lifetime. In fact, if your mission can be completed in your lifetime, it isn't a big enough mission" (301).

92. John 10:4, 27.

CHAPTER 5

93. Romans 7:14–25.

94. This paragraph references various texts in Romans 8.

95. Fee, *First Epistle to the Corinthians*, 5.

96. Fee, *First Epistle to the Corinthians*, 11.

97. As noted below, Paul refers to them as "super apostles" (2 Cor 11:5, 13; 12:11).

98. 1 Corinthians 4:7–10.

99. 1 Corinthians 3:18b–19a.

100. 1 Corinthians 1:18–31.

101. 1 Corinthians 4:16; 11:1.

102. Paul asks Christians to "imitate" him (1 Cor 4:16; 11:1; Eph 5:1; 1 Thess 1:6; 2:14) and to follow his "example" (Phil 3:17; 2 Thess 3:7, 9; 2 Tim 1:13).

103. 1 Corinthians 2:4–5.

104. Womble, "Key Terms in Books: 2 Corinthians."

105. 2 Corinthians 11:5, 13; 12:11.

106. 2 Corinthians 11:13–15.

107. 2 Corinthians 11:14.

ENDNOTES

108. 2 Corinthians 11:18.
109. Baker, *2 Corinthians*, 28.
110. 2 Corinthians 11:4.
111. Baker, *2 Corinthians*, 28.
112. Galatians 1:6–7.
113. Galatians 3:1–3.
114. Galatians 4:9b.
115. Galatians 5:1.
116. Ephesians 6:10–18.
117. Philippians 1:27; 2:2, 14; 4:2.
118. Philippians 1:28; 3:2, 18.
119. Philippians 1:15, 17.
120. Arndt, Gingrich, Danker, & Bauer, *Greek-English Lexicon of the New Testament*, 309.
121. Fee, *Paul's Letter to the Philippians*, 119.
122. Colossians 1:9; 2:3.
123. Colossians 2:2; 3:10.
124. Womble, "Key Terms in Books: Colossians."
125. Colossians 2:8–23.
126. Colossians 2:10.
127. Acts 17:1–10.
128. 1 Thessalonians 1:6; 2:14.
129. 1 Thessalonians 1:7.
130. 1 Thessalonians 2:13.
131. Womble, "Key Terms in Books: 1 Thessalonians."
132. 1 Thessalonians 5:15.
133. 1 Thessalonians 2:2; 3:4.
134. 1 Thessalonians 2:14.
135. 1 Thessalonians 2:16.
136. 2 Thessalonians 1:4–5.
137. 2 Thessalonians 2:15.
138. 2 Thessalonians 5:15.

Endnotes

139. 1 Timothy 1:3–7; 6:3–4, 20–21.
140. Womble, "Key Terms in Books: 1 Timothy."
141. 1 Timothy 1:4, 6; 6:4, 20.
142. 1 Timothy 6:20.
143. 1 Timothy 1:7; 6:4.
144. 1 Timothy 6:3.
145. 1 Timothy 6:21, also see 1:19; 4:1; 6:10.
146. 1 Timothy 6:12; 1:18–19.
147. 1 Timothy 2:2; 3:16; 4:7, 8; 6:3, 5, 6, 11, and 2:10 in NASB.
148. Womble, "Key Terms in Books: 1 Timothy." See 1 Timothy 1:16; 2:2, 9–10; 3:2–16; 4:12, 15; 5:4–10, 25; 6:1–2, 12.
149. Titus 1:5.
150. Titus 1:10, 14; 3:9.
151. 1 Timothy 1:7 and Titus 1:10, 14; 3:9.
152. 1 Timothy 6:5 and Titus 1:11.
153. Titus 1:1; 2:12.
154. Titus 1:16; 2:7, 14; 3:1, 8, 14.
155. Titus 1:16.
156. Titus 3:14.
157. 1 Timothy 6:4 and 2 Timothy 2:14.
158. 1 Timothy 6:20 and 2 Timothy 2:16.
159. 1 Timothy 1:4 and 2 Timothy 2:23.
160. 1 Timothy 5:13–15 and 2 Timothy 3:6.
161. Towner, *Letters to Timothy and Titus*, 626.
162. Towner, *Letters to Timothy and Titus*, 39.
163. 2 Timothy 1:15; 2:17; 4:10, 16.
164. 2 Timothy 1:13.
165. 2 Timothy 1:14.
166. 2 Timothy 2:1.
167. 2 Timothy 2:2–6.
168. 2 Timothy 2:15.
169. 2 Timothy 2:22.

Endnotes

170. 2 Timothy 3:14.

171. 2 Timothy 4:5.

172. Philemon 1, 9–10, 13, 23.

173. Philemon 1.

174. Womble, "Key Terms in Books: Philemon."

175. Simmons, "22 Hilariously Bad Pieces of Advice."

CHAPTER 6

176. New 2023 MLB rules limit pitchers to "two disengagements (pickoff attempts or step-offs) per plate appearance. However, this limit is reset if a runner or runners advance during the plate appearance. If a third pickoff attempt is made, the runner automatically advances one base if the pickoff attempt is not successful." Castrovince, "Pitch Timer."

177. 1 Peter 1:1.

178. 1 Peter 5:4.

179. 1 Peter 5:7.

180. Matthew 4:1–11 and Luke 4:1–13.

181. Matthew 4:11.

182. Luke 4:13.

183. Matthew 4:18–22.

184. John 6:64, 70–71.

185. John 12:4–6.

186. John 13:27.

187. John 14:22.

188. Matthew 7:21–23.

189. Schilder, *Christ in His Suffering*, 173.

190. Schilder, *Christ in His Suffering*, 188.

191. Henderson stole 41 bases during the 1987 season but only played in 95 games (.431 per game). Thus, if he had played 150 games, we may guess that he would have stolen 65 bases. So, if he had been healthy, he may have stolen a total of 467, still 82 bags short of Coleman.

192. Monagan has a great article on this event, which includes the video sequence. Monagan, "After 17 Pickoff Throws."

193. Matthew 17:1–8; Mark 9:2–8 and Luke 9:28–36.

ENDNOTES

CHAPTER 7

194. That's the story that's been told since the 1940s, when the event was "embellished." According to the Sporting News, Ruth was actually cut down on a hit and run. Dan Holmes says, "It's important to note that newspaper accounts of the game, where they detailed the game action, never called Ruth's play a 'caught stealing' and at the time they did not criticize Ruth's conduct." He adds, "It was a play to get the runner moving in a situation where the Yankees desperately needed a run against a pitcher [Grover Cleveland Alexander] who had dominated them." Apparently, the batter, Bob Meusel signaled to Ruth for the hit and run but then swung and missed the pitch. Holmes, "Babe Ruth's Failed Stolen Base Attempt."

195. Tietz, *Karl Barth*, 211.

196. Tietz, *Karl Barth*, 211.

197. Tietz, *Karl Barth*, 211.

198. Tietz, *Karl Barth*, 211.

199. Tietz, *Karl Barth*, 211.

200. Tietz, *Karl Barth*, 211, 231.

201. Tietz, *Karl Barth*, 213.

202. I understand the argument about giving outs away, but putting the ball in play doesn't always lead to an out anyway. A ground ball may lead to an error or even a hit.

203. In 1925, Meusel led the A.L. in both HR (33) and RBI (134). In case you're wondering, the Babe only played 98 games that year.

204. For 56 years, Gehrig's consecutive games played streak of 2,130 stood. Only the crippling ALS disease could take Gehrig out of the lineup. Cal Ripken Jr. still holds the record of 2,632 consecutive games played.

205. Murray, "All Rose Could Do Was Hustle."

CHAPTER 8

206. Sweet, *Jesus Human*, 84.

207. Baseball Reference, "Willie Mays."

208. ESPN Classic, "Willie Mays—Sports Century."

209. Schleier, "You'll Strike Out in Life."

210. Schleier, "You'll Strike Out in Life."

211. Schleier, "You'll Strike Out in Life."

ENDNOTES

212. TSN Archives, "Willie Mays is Still Having Fun."

213. As an example, the NASB20 says "imitate" in 1 Corinthians 11:1.

214. Sweet, *Jesus Human*, 207.

215. Genesis 1:10, 12, 18, 21, 25, 31

216. Despite being imprisoned (Phil 1:7, 13–14, 17), Paul's big theme in Philippians is that we can always "rejoice" (9x) and have "joy" (7x).

217. 1 Peter 5:7

218. Matthew 6:25–34.

219. Matthew 6:32.

220. Philippians 4:6.

221. Matthew 6:26.

222. *Frasier*, "Cranes Go Caribbean."

223. Betts was the 2018 A.L. MVP and is a 3x runner-up (2016, 2020, 2023).

CHAPTER 9

224. Matthew 7:24–27.

225. Stott, *Message of The Sermon on the Mount*, 209.

226. Colossians 2:6.

227. Sweet, *Designer Jesus*, 65.

228. Matthew 7:21.

229. Sweet, *Designer Jesus*, 45.

230. A double play.

231. Matthew 28:19.

232. Colossians 1:6.

233. Philippians 4:14–19.

CHAPTER 10

234. Philippians 2:25; 2 Timothy 2:3; Philemon 2.

235. In 2021, the film titled *Operation Mincemeat* starring Colin Firth was released.

236. Tripney, "Operation Mincemeat."

ENDNOTES

237. Tripney, "Operation Mincemeat."

238. Andrews, "What Was Operation Mincemeat?"

239. Tripney, "Operation Mincemeat."

240. Tripney, "Operation Mincemeat."

241. Andrews, "What Was Operation Mincemeat?"

242. Wikipedia, "Battle of the Little Bighorn."

243. History.com editors, "Battle of the Little Bighorn."

244. NPS.gov, "Chronology of the Battle of the Little Bighorn."

245. NPS.gov, "Chronology of the Battle of the Little Bighorn."

246. NPS.gov, "Chronology of the Battle of the Little Bighorn."

247. History.com editors, "Battle of the Little Bighorn."

248. History.com editors, "Battle of the Little Bighorn."

249. Wikipedia, "Battle of the Little Bighorn."

250. John 10:10; 1 Pet 5:8.

251. The Editors of Encyclopedia Britannica, "Battles of Trenton and Princeton." Green, "The 9 Most Memorable Surprise Attacks."

252. Green, "The 9 Most Memorable Surprise Attacks."

253. Green, "The 9 Most Memorable Surprise Attacks."

254. The Editors of Encyclopedia Britannica, "Battles of Trenton and Princeton."

255. Green, "The 9 Most Memorable Surprise Attacks."

256. The Editors of Encyclopedia Britannica, "Battles of Trenton and Princeton."

257. History.com editors, "Battle of Gettysburg."

258. History.com editors, "Battle of Gettysburg."

259. The Editors of Encyclopedia Britannica, "The Battle of Gettysburg."

260. The Editors of Encyclopedia Britannica, "The Battle of Gettysburg."

261. Mike D., "Why Lee Didn't Listen to Longstreet."

262. History.com editors, "Battle of Gettysburg."

263. History.com editors, "Battle of Gettysburg."

264. Mike D., "Why Lee Didn't Listen to Longstreet."

265. Shaara, "Critical Essays."

266. Shaara, "Critical Essays."

Endnotes

267. Shaara, "Critical Essays."

268. Klein, "Fooling Hitler."

269. Klein, "Fooling Hitler."

270. History.com editors, "D-Day."

271. Rowe, "The Greatest Deceptions in Military History."

272. Beyond the misinformation, the Allies also used elaborate deceptive tactics (serving as further examples for chapter 1). These tactics included: phantom fighting forces headed by General George Patton, dummy aircraft, decoy landing crafts, inflatable Sherman tanks, stepped up aerial attacks to mislead the Nazis, false radar readings, using a look-alike actor to impersonate a British general, and even dropping "dummy paratroopers that were wired to simulate the sounds of rifle fire and grenades when they hit the ground." Klein, "Fooling Hitler."

273. Klein, "Fooling Hitler."

274. Klein, "Fooling Hitler."

275. Klein, "Fooling Hitler."

276. Rowe, "The Greatest Deceptions in Military History."

277. Klein, "Fooling Hitler."

278. Klein, "Fooling Hitler."

279. Holland, "History Vault: Operation Desert Storm."

280. Holland, "History Vault: Operation Desert Storm."

281. U. S. History, "60a. Operation Desert Storm."

282. Deptula, "Desert Storm at 30."

283. Deptula, "Desert Storm at 30."

CONCLUSION

284. WAR stands for wins above replacement and ERA stands for earned run average over nine innings pitched.

285. John 10:1–18, 25–30.

286. Arndt, Gingrich, Danker, & Bauer, *Greek-English Lexicon of the New Testament*, 109.

287. John 10:27.

288. James 1:23.

289. John 10:12.

APPENDIX A

NT References to Satan

(NASB95)

NUMBER OF REFERENCES TO SATAN

Satan (36x)
devil (34x)
Beelzebul or Beelzebub (7x)
the evil one (7x + 1?)
deceiver (4x)
ruler of the demons (3x)
ruler of this world (3x)
serpent or serpent of old (3x)
tempter (2x)
the accuser (1x)
god of this world (1x)
he who is in the world (1x)
prince of the power of the air (1x)

MATTHEW

Satan—4:10; 12:26; 16:23
devil—4:1, 5, 8, 11; 13:39; 25:41
Beelzebul—10:25; 12:24, 27
tempter—4:3
the evil one—*5:37?*; 13:19

ruler of the demons—12:24

MARK

Satan—1:13; 3:23, 26; 4:15; 8:33
Beelzebul—3:22
ruler of the demons—3:22

LUKE

Satan—10:18; 11:18; 13:16; 22:3, 31
devil—4:2-3, 6, 13; 8:12
Beelzebul—11:15, 18-19
ruler of the demons—11:15

JOHN

Satan—13:27
devil—6:70; 8:44; 13:2
ruler of this world—12:31; 14:30; 16:11
the evil one—17:15
thief—10:10 (contextually, also used of false teachers)

ACTS

Satan—5:3; 26:18
devil—10:38; 13:10

ROMANS

Satan—16:20

1 CORINTHIANS

Satan—5:5; 7:5

2 CORINTHIANS

Satan—2:11; 11:14; 12:7
god of this world—4:4

serpent/deceiver—11:3

EPHESIANS

devil—4:27; 6:11
prince of the power of the air—2:2

1 THESSALONIANS

Satan—2:18
tempter—3:5

2 THESSALONIANS

Satan—2:9
the evil one—3:2

1 TIMOTHY

Satan—1:20; 5:15
Deceiver—2:14
devil—3:6-7

2 TIMOTHY

devil—2:26

HEBREWS

devil—2:14

JAMES

devil—4:7

1 PETER

devil—5:8

APPENDIX A

1 JOHN

devil—3:8, 10
he who is in the world—4:4
the evil one—2:13; 3:12; 5:18–19

JUDE

devil—9

REVELATION

Satan—2:9, 13, 24; 3:9; 12:9; 20:2, 7
devil—2:10; 12:9, 12; 20:2, 10
deceiver—12:9; 20:2-3
the accuser—12:10
serpent of old—12:9; 20:2

APPENDIX B

NT References to Demons

(NASB95)

REFERENCES TO DEMONS

demons (80x)
unclean spirits (22x)
rulers, authorities, dominion, angels, principalities, powers (9x)
spiritual forces of wickedness (1x)

MATTHEW

demons—7:22; 8:16, 28, 31; 9:32-34; 10:8; 11:18; 12:22-28; 15:22; 17:18
unclean spirit—10:1; 12:43

MARK

demons—1:32-39; 3:15, 22; 5:12-18; 6:13; 7:26-30; 9:38; 16:9, 17
unclean spirit—1:23, 26-27; 3:11, 30; 5:2, 8; 6:7; 7:25; 9:25

LUKE

demons—4:33-34; 7:33; 8:2, 27-38; 9:42, 49; 10:17; 11:14-20; 13:32
unclean spirit—4:33, 36; 6:18; 8:29; 9:42; 11:24

JOHN
demons—7:20; 8:48-49, 52; 10:20-21

ACTS
unclean spirit—5:16; 8:7

ROMANS
angels, principalities, powers—8:38

1 CORINTHIANS
demons—10:20-21
rule, authority, power—15:24

EPHESIANS
rule, authority, power, dominion—1:21
rulers & authorities—3:10
rulers, powers, forces of darkness, spiritual forces of wickedness—6:12

COLOSSIANS
thrones, dominions, rulers & authorities—1:16; 2:15

1 TIMOTHY
demons—4:1

JAMES
demons—2:19; 3:15

1 PETER
angels, authorities, powers—3:22

REVELATION
demons—9:20; 16:14; 18:2
unclean spirits—16:13; 18:2

APPENDIX C

Warnings of Deception

(NASB95)

Warnings of deception are mentioned either explicitly or implicitly in 23 of 27 books (not in: John, 1 Cor, 1 Thess, Phlm).

MATTHEW

- 4:1-11—the devil tempting Jesus
- 7:15—"Beware of false prophets, who come to you in sheep's clothing, but inwardly are ravenous wolves."
- 10:16—"I send you out as sheep in the midst of wolves."
- 13:22—"deceitfulness of riches choke the word"
- 13:38-41—"the tares are the sons of the evil one, and the enemy who sowed them is the devil . . . stumbling blocks"
- 15:14—the Pharisees are "blind guides to the blind"
- 16:6-12—beware of the teaching of the Pharisees and Sadducees
- 23:16, 24—the Pharisees are "blind guides"
- 24:4-5—"See to it that no one misleads you. For many will come in My name, saying, 'I am the Christ, and will mislead many.'"
- 24:11—"Many false prophets will arise and will mislead many."

WARNINGS OF DECEPTION

- 24:24—"For false Christs and false prophets will arise and will show great signs and wonders, so as to mislead, if possible, even the elect."

MARK

- 1:13—Jesus tempted by Satan
- 4:3-20 (parable of sower)—Satan takes away the word sown . . . "affliction and persecution" . . . deceitfulness of riches and desires" choke the word
- 7:8—deceived by traditions
- 8:33—not setting our mind on God's interests is a means for being deceived
- 12:38-40—"Beware of the scribes"
- 13:5-6—"Many will come in My name, saying, 'I am He!' and will mislead many."
- 13:21-22—"false Christs and false prophets will arise"

LUKE

- 4:1-13—Jesus tempted by the devil
- 6:26—false prophets *(of old)*
- 8:4-15—(parable of sower)—devil comes and takes away the word from their heart
- 11:39-52—leaders who deceive
- 17:1—stumbling blocks

ACTS

- 20:29-30—savage wolves will come in . . . speak perverse things

APPENDIX C

ROMANS

- 16:17-18—"keep your eye on those who cause dissensions and hindrances contrary to the teaching which you learned"

2 CORINTHIANS

- 2:11—"by Satan, for we are not ignorant of his schemes"
- 4:4—"the god of this world has blinded the minds of the unbelieving so that they might not see the light of the gospel of the glory of Christ"
- 11:14-15—"No wonder, for even Satan disguises himself as an angel of light. Therefore, it is not surprising if his servants also disguise themselves as servants of righteousness, whose end will be according to their deeds."
- 11:26—false brethren
- 12:7—"a messenger of Satan"

GALATIANS

- 1:7—"only there are some who are disturbing you and want to distort the gospel of Christ."
- 2:4—"But *it was* because of the false brethren."
- 3:1—"You foolish Galatians, who has bewitched you?"

EPHESIANS

- 2:2-3a—"you formerly walked ... according to the prince of the power of the air, of the spirit that is now working in the sons of disobedience. Among them we too all formerly lived in the lusts of our flesh, indulging the desires of the flesh and of the mind."
- 4:14—deceitful scheming
- 5:6—"let no one deceive you with empty words"

WARNINGS OF DECEPTION

- 6:11—"schemes of the devil"
- 6:12—"our struggle is against spiritual forces of wickedness"

PHILIPPIANS

- 1:15, 17—"Some, to be sure, are preaching Christ even from envy and strife . . . proclaim Christ out of selfish ambition rather than from pure motives."
- 3:2–3a—"Beware of the dogs, beware of the evil workers, beware of the false circumcision; for we are the *true* circumcision." (Bruce says they are probably all the same group, the Jews)—those who put confidence in their heritage.
- 3:18–19—"For many walk . . . *they are* enemies of the cross of Christ, whose end is destruction, whose god is *their* appetite, and *whose* glory is in their shame, who set their minds on earthly things."

COLOSSIANS

- 2:4—"no one will delude you with persuasive argument"
- 2:8—"See to it that no one takes you captive through philosophy and empty deception."
- 2:16–23—legalistic activities . . . activities leading to greater spirituality—"Let no one disqualify you, insisting on asceticism and worship of angels, going on in detail about visions." (ESV)

2 THESSALONIANS

- Deception (2:3, 10)

APPENDIX C

1 TIMOTHY

- 1:3—"As I urged you upon my departure for Macedonia, remain on at Ephesus so that you may instruct certain men not to teach strange doctrines."
- 4:1-2—"But the Spirit explicitly says that in later times some will fall away from the faith, paying attention to deceitful spirits and doctrines of demons."
- 6:3-5—"If anyone advocates a different doctrine and does not agree with sound words, those of our Lord Jesus Christ, and with the doctrine conforming to godliness, he is conceited *and* understands nothing; but he has a morbid interest in controversial questions and disputes about words, out of which arise envy, strife, abusive language, evil suspicions, and constant friction between men of depraved mind and deprived of the truth, who suppose that godliness is a means of gain."

2 TIMOTHY

- 2:16-18—"But avoid worldly *and* empty chatter, for it will lead to further ungodliness, and their talk will spread."
- 3:1-5—"But realize this, that in the last days difficult times will come. For men will be lovers of self, lovers of money, boastful, arrogant, revilers, disobedient to parents, ungrateful, unholy, unloving, irreconcilable, malicious gossips, without self-control, brutal, haters of good, treacherous, reckless, conceited, lovers of pleasure rather than lovers of God, holding to a form of godliness, although they have denied its power."
- 3:13—"But evil men and impostors will proceed *from bad* to worse, deceiving and being deceived."
- 4:3-4—"For the time will come when they will not endure sound doctrine; but *wanting* to have their ears tickled, they will accumulate for themselves teachers in accordance to their own desires, and will turn away their ears from the truth and will turn aside to myths."

Warnings of Deception

TITUS

- 1:10-16—"For there are many rebellious men, empty talkers and deceivers... They profess to know God, but by *their* deeds they deny *Him*, being detestable and disobedient and worthless for any good deed."
- 3:3—"For we also once were foolish ourselves, disobedient, deceived, enslaved to various lusts and pleasures, spending our life in malice and envy, hateful, hating one another."

HEBREWS

- 4:12—An implicit message of "falling away"
- 6:1-6—An implicit message of "falling away"
- 10:26-39—An implicit message of "throwing away" confidence
- 13:9—strange teachings

JAMES

- 4:4—"You adulteresses, do you not know that friendship with the world is hostility toward God? Therefore whoever wishes to be a friend of the world makes himself an enemy of God."

1 PETER

- 5:8—"Be of sober *spirit*, be on the alert. Your adversary, the devil, prowls around like a roaring lion, seeking someone to devour."

2 PETER

- 2:12—reviling where they have no knowledge
- All of chapter 2: false prophets, destructive heresies, follow their sensuality, greed, false words, indulge the flesh, reveling in their

APPENDIX C

deceptions, forsaking the right way, speaking out arrogant words of vanity they entice by fleshly desires.

- 3:16—regarding teaching—the untaught and unstable distort
- 3:17—"be on your guard so that you are not carried away by the error of unprincipled men"

1 JOHN

- 2:26—"These things I have written to you concerning those who are trying to deceive you." (also 3:7)
- "False prophets" (4:1) and "antichrists" (2:18, 22; 4:3)

2 JOHN

- "Truth" (5x) is the most important term in this short letter, as John contrasts truth with "deceivers" who do not abide in the teachings of Christ (vv. 7-10).
- Verses 7-9—"For many deceivers have gone out into the world, those who do not acknowledge Jesus Christ *as* coming in the flesh. This is the deceiver and the antichrist. Watch yourselves, that you do not lose what we have accomplished, but that you may receive a full reward. Anyone who goes too far and does not abide in the teaching of Christ, does not have God; the one who abides in the teaching, he has both the Father and the Son."

3 JOHN

- "Truth" (6x plus "true" 1x) is the key word in 3 John. Gaius (v. 3), Demetrius (v. 12) and, of course John, walk in the truth. This is set in opposition to Diotrephes (vv. 10-11) who clearly does not.

WARNINGS OF DECEPTION

JUDE

- Jude warns the church against "ungodly" (6x) persons who "have crept in unnoticed . . . who turn the grace of our God into licentiousness" (v. 4)—(the NIV says, "who pervert the grace of our God into a license for immorality").

- v. 16—"These are grumblers, finding fault, following after their *own* lusts; they speak arrogantly, flattering people for the sake of *gaining an* advantage."

REVELATION

- chapters 2–3—we might say 6 of 7 churches have been deceived in some way
- 2:1–7 (Ephesus)—deeds but have lost first love in Christ
- 2:8–11 (Smyrna)—false Jews who are of synagogue of Satan
- 2:12–17 (Pergamum)—false teaching
- 2:18–29 (Thyatira)—false teaching
- 3:1–6 (Sardis)—think they are alive, but are dead
- 3:14–22 (Laodicea)—lukewarm
- 12:9—Satan, who deceives the whole world
- 16:13–14—the false prophet
- 19:20—false prophet who deceived those who had received the mark of the beast (mentioned other places in Rev—e.g., 13:16–17)
- 20:2–3—Satan thrown into the abyss so that he would not deceive the nations any longer
- 20:7–8—Satan released and will come out to deceive the nations
- 20:10—devil who deceived them was thrown into the lake of fire where the beast and false prophet also reside
- 21:8; 22:15—sorcerers and liars (they may be considered deceivers)

Bibliography

Andrews, Evan. "What Was Operation Mincemeat?" Updated September 28, 2023. https://www.history.com/news/what-was-operation-mincemeat.

Arndt, W., F. W. Gingrich, F. W. Danker, & W. Bauer. *A Greek-English Lexicon of the New Testament and Other Early Christian Literature: A Translation and Adaption of the fourth revised and augmented edition of Walter Bauer's Griechisch-deutsches Worterbuch zu den Schrift en des Neuen Testaments und der ubrigen urchristlichen Literatur*. Chicago: University of Chicago Press, 1979.

Baker, William R. *2 Corinthians*. The College Press NIV Commentary. Joplin, MO: College Press, 1999.

Baseball-Reference.com. "Pitching Season & Career Finder." https://www.baseball-reference.com/play-index/tiny.fcgi?id=jmMP4.

Bernier, Doug. "Base Running 4: Tips for Leading off First Base, Second Base, and Secondary Leads." n. d. https://probaseballinsider.com/baseball-instruction/base-running/how-to-take-a-lead-at-1st-and-2nd-base/.

Castrovince, Anthony. "Pitch Timer, Shift Restrictions Among Announced Rule Changes for '23." MLB, February 1, 2023. https://www.mlb.com/news/mlb-2023-rule-changes-pitch-timer-larger-bases-shifts.

D., Mike. "Why Lee Didn't Listen to Longstreet." n.d. https://www.americancivilwarforum.com/why-lee-didnt-listen-to-longstreet...79594.html.

Deptula, David. "Desert Storm at 30: Aerospace Power and the U.S. Military." March 1, 2021. https://warontherocks.com/2021/03/desert-storm-at-30-aerospace-power-and-the-u-smilitary/.

Encyclopedia Britannica editors. "The Battle of Gettysburg." Updated December 5, 2023 by Adam Augustyn. https://www.britannica.com/event/Battle-of-Gettysburg.

———. "Battles of Trenton and Princeton." n.d. https://www.britannica.com/event/Battles-of-Trenton-and-Princeton.

ESPN Classic. "Willie Mays—Sports Century."

Fee, Gordon D. *The First Epistle to the Corinthians*. The New International Commentary on the New Testament. Grand Rapids: Eerdmans, 2014.

BIBLIOGRAPHY

———. *Paul's Letter to the Philippians*. The New International Commentary on the New Testament. Grand Rapids: Eerdmans, 1995.

Frasier. Season 8, Episode 23, "Cranes Go Caribbean."

Green, Alan. "The 9 Most Memorable Surprise Attacks That Caught the Enemy Off Guard." May 25, 2021. https://www.historynet.com/the-9-most-memorable-surprise-attacks-that-caught-the-enemy-off-guard/.

Hess, Richard S. *Joshua: An Introduction and Commentary*. Tyndale Old Testament Commentaries 6. Downers Grove, IL: InterVarsity, 1996.

History.com editors. "Battle of Gettysburg." Updated March 17, 2023. https://www.history.com/topics/american-civil-war/battle-of-gettysburg.

———. "Battle of the Little Bighorn." Updated December 21, 2020. https://www.history.com/topics/native-american-history/battle-of-the-little-bighorn.

———. "D-Day." Updated May 11, 2023. https://www.history.com/topics/world-war-ii/d-day.

Holland, Brynn. "History Vault: Operation Desert Storm." Updated August 23, 2018. https://www.history.com/news/history-vault-operation-desert-storm.

Holmes, Dan. "Babe Ruth's Failed Stolen Base Attempt Ended The 1926 World Series, Or Did It?" October 30, 2019. https://baseballegg.com/2019/10/30/babe-ruths-failed-stolen-base-attempt-ended-the-1926-world-series-or-is-that-what-really-happened/.

Kepner, Tyler. "Pickoff Tips from James Shields." May 21, 2011. https://archive.nytimes.com/bats.blogs.nytimes.com/2011/05/21/pickoff-tips-from-james-shields/.

King Jr., Martin Luther. "Love of Enemy." In *Following the Call: Living the Sermon on the Mount Together*, edited by Charles E. Moore. New York: Plough, 2021.

Klein, Christopher. "Fooling Hitler: The Elaborate Ruse Behind D-Day." Updated June 27, 2023. https://www.history.com/news/fooling-hitler-the-elaborate-ruse-behind-d-day.

Koptak, Paul E. *Proverbs*. The NIV Application Commentary. Grand Rapids: Zondervan, 2003.

McNeal, Reggie. *Missional Renaissance: Changing the Scorecard for the Church*. San Francisco: Jossey-Bass, 2009.

MLB. "1974 WS Gm2: Marshall Picks Off Washington in Ninth." YouTube video, July 18, 2013. https://www.youtube.com/watch?v=vWb8oQz75bk.

———. "SD@TOR: Dickey Catches Myers leaning in the 1st." YouTube video, July 27, 2016. https://www.youtube.com/watch?v=qT_9anQikgI.

———. "Willians Astudillo Picks Off Shane Robinson Without Even Looking!" YouTube video, Mar. 13, 2018. https://www.youtube.com/watch?v=3JG-ZnnqSWw.

Monagan, Matt. "After 17 Pickoff Throws, He Still Stole Second." January 14, 2022. https://www.mlb.com/news/vince-coleman-drew-most-pickoff-throws-ever.

BIBLIOGRAPHY

Muder, Craig. "Bench's Excellence Wraps Up Reds' Second Straight Title." https://baseballhall.org/discover/inside-pitch/johnny-bench-excellence-wraps-up-reds-second-straight-title.

Murphy, Roland E. *Proverbs*. Word Biblical Commentary 22. Nashville: Thomas Nelson, 1998.

Murray, Jim. "All Rose Could Do Was Hustle—Right to the Top." *Los Angeles Times*, September 8, 1985. https://www.latimes.com/archives/la-xpm-1985-09-08-sp-3025-story.html.

Muskat, Carrie. "Lester Tested, Foils Strategy with Rare Pickoff." MLB, June 3, 2017. https://www.mlb.com/news/cubs-jon-lester-picks-off-tommy-pham-at-first-c234175336.

NPS.gov. "A Chronology of the Battle of the Little Bighorn." Updated March 10, 2023. https://www.nps.gov/libi/learn/a-chronology-of-the-battle-of-the-little-bighorn.htm.

Rowe, Richard. "The Greatest Deceptions in Military History." September 23, 2021. https://www.ranker.com/list/deceptions-in-military-history/richard-rowe.

Schilder, Klass. *Christ in His Suffering*. 2nd ed. Minneapolis: Klock & Klock, 1978.

Schleier, Curt. "You'll Strike Out in Life, Unless You Follow Willie May's Advice." July 23, 2020. https://www.investors.com/news/management/leaders-and-success/willie-mays-bio-key-success-have-fun/.

Shaara, Michael. "Critical Essays: The Lee Versus Longstreet Battle Strategy Conflict." n.d. https://www.cliffsnotes.com/literature/k/the-killer-angels/critical-essays/the-lee-versus-longstreet-battle-strategy-conflict.

Simmons, Andy. "22 Hilariously Bad Pieces of Advice You Shouldn't Follow." Updated January 31, 2023. https://www.rd.com/article/hilariously-bad-advice/.

Stott, John R. W. *The Message of The Sermon on the Mount*. Downers Grove: InterVarsity, 1978.

Sweet, Leonard. *Aqua Church 2.0*. Colorado Springs: David C. Cook, 1999.

———. *Designer Jesus: The Lifestory of a Disciple*. Absecon, NJ: Salish Sea, 2024.

———. *I Am a Follower: The Way, the Truth, and the Life of Following Jesus*. Nashville: Thomas Nelson, 2012.

———. *Jesus Human: Primer for Common Humanity*. Absecon, NJ: Salish Sea, 2023.

Tietz, Christiane. *Karl Barth: A Life in Conflict*. Oxford: Oxford University Press, 2021.

Towner, Philip H. *The Letters to Timothy and Titus*. The New International Commentary on the New Testament. Grand Rapids: Eerdmans, 2006.

Tripney, Natasha. "Operation Mincemeat: The Incredible Plot that Tricked Hitler." BBC, April 18, 2022. https://www.bbc.com/culture/article/20220414-operation-mincemeat-the-incredible-plot-that-tricked-hitler.

Bibliography

TSN Archives, "Willie Mays is Still Having Fun (July 25, 1970, issue)." November 8, 2022. https://www.sportingnews.com/us/mlb/news/tsn-archives-willie-mays-still-having-fun-july-25-1970-issue/jtydwifrsgewvdbv7iliu5fo.

U.S. History. "60a. Operation Desert Storm." https://www.ushistory.org/us/60a.asp.

Wikipedia. "Battle of the Little Bighorn." https://en.wikipedia.org/wiki/Battle_of_the_Little_Bighorn.

Womble, T. Scott. *Beyond Reasonable Doubt: 95 Theses Which Dispute the Church's Conviction Against Women*. USA: Xulon, 2008.

———. "Key Terms in Books." *NT Repetition Study Bible*. https://tscottwomble.com/nt-repetition-study-bible/book-themes/.

Scripture Index

OLD TESTAMENT

Genesis
1:10	130n215
1:12	130n215
1:18	130n215
1:21	130n215
1:25	130n215
1:31	130n215
3:13	5

Deuteronomy
4	52
7:1–6	46
7:1	46

Joshua
1:1–5	45, 124n79
6	45
8	45
9:1–2	124n80
9:3–15	124n81
9:7	124n82
9:14–15	45
9:17	124n83

Judges
13:1–16:31	123n44
13:24	25
16:1	25
16:7	123n45
16:11	123n45
16:13	123n45
16:15	25
16:16	25
16:17	25

2 Samuel
21:1–6	124n84

1 Kings
15:11–1	47

2 Chronicles
16:12–13	47

Proverbs
3:1–12	44

NEW TESTAMENT

Matthew
4:1–11	128n180, 140
4:1	133

Scripture Index

Matthew (continued)

4:3	133
4:5	133
4:8	133
4:10	133
4:11	128n181, 133
4:18–22	128n183
5:1–7:29	122n18
5:14	122n19
5:16	122n20–21
5:21–48	25
5:29	123n46
5:37	133
5:44	122n24
6:9–13	35
6:25–34	130n218
6:26	130n221
6:32	130n219
7:1–5	17
7:7	122n28
7:11	122n29
7:15–23	16, 58
7:15	121n5, 140
7:21–23	128n188
7:21	130n228
7:22	137
7:24–27	130n224
8:16	137
8:28	137
8:31	137
9:32–34	137
10:1	137
10:8	137
10:16	140
10:25	133
11:18	137
12:22–28	137
12:24	133
12:26	133
12:27	133
12:43	137
13:19	133
13:22	140
13:38–41	140
13:39	133
15:14	140
15:22	137
16:6–12	140
16:23	133
17:1–8	128n193
17:5	77
17:18	137
23:16	140
23:24	140
24:4–5	140
24:11	140
24:24	141
25:41	133
28:19–20	34
28:19	130n231

Mark

1:13	134, 141
1:23	137
1:26–27	137
1:32–39	137
3:11	137
3:15	137
3:22	134
3:23	134
3:26	134
3:30	137
4:3–20	141
4:15	134
5:1–20	72
5:2	137
5:8	137
5:12–18	137
6:7	137
6:13	137
7:8	141
7:25	137
7:26–30	137
8:33	134, 141
9:2–8	128n193
9:25	137
9:38	137
12:38–40	141

Scripture Index

13:5–6	141	7:20	138
13:21–22	141	8:44	121n4, 134
16:9	137	8:48–49	138
16:17	137	8:52	138
		10:1–18	132n285
Luke		10:4	125n92
		10:7	124n64
4:1–13	128n180, 141	10:8	118
4:2–3	134	10:9	124n64
4:6	134	10:10	118, 131n250, 134
4:13	128n182, 134		
4:33–34	137	10:12	132n289
4:33	137	10:20–21	138
4:36	137	10:25–30	118, 132n285
6:18	137	10:27	121n12, 125n92, 132n287
6:26	141		
7:33	137		
8:2	137	10:28–29	118
8:4–15	121n7, 141	12:4–6	128n185
8:12	134	12:31	134
8:27–38	137	13:2	124n67, 134
8:29	137	13:27	124n67, 128n186, 134
9:28–36	128n193		
9:42	137	14:6	121n6, 124n63, n70
9:49	137		
10:17	137	14:22	128n187
10:18	134	14:30	134
11:14–20	137	16:11	134
11:15	134	17:1–26	35
11:18	134	17:11–12	124n66
11:24	137	17:11	124n68
11:39–52	141	17:12	124n67
13:10–17	72	17:13	124n71
13:16	134	17:15	124n66, 134
13:32	137	17:17	124n69
17:1	141	17:19	124n69
18–19	134	17:21–23	124n68
22:3	124n67, 134	17:21	124n66
22:31	134	17:23–24	124n66
		17:26	124n72
John			
		Acts	
6:64	128n184		
6:70–71	128n184	1:1–11	124n65
6:70	134	5:3	134

Acts (continued)

5:16	138
8:7	138
10:38	134
13:10	134
17:1–10	126n127
20:25	123n55
20:28–31	30, 123n52, n54
20:29–30	141
20:31	33
20:36	123n56
20:38	123n55
26:18	134

Romans

4:11	125n89
4:16	125n89
5:10	122n27
6:1–23	123n43
6:1–2	122n31
6:6	55
6:7	55
6:17	55
6:18	55
6:20	55
6:22	55
7:14–25	125n93
8:1–39	55, 125n94
8:38	138
16:17–18	142
16:20	134

1 Corinthians

1:18–31	125n100
2:4–5	125n103
3:18–19	125n99
4:7–10	125n98
4:16	125n101–2
5:5	134
7:5	134
9:24–26	8
10:20–21	138
11:1	125n101–2, 130n213
15:24	138
16:10–19	30
16:13	30, 33, 123n52

2 Corinthians

1:15–17	57
2:11	123n40, 134, 142
4:4	123n39, 134, 142
11:3	5, 135
11:4	126n110
11:5	125n105
11:6	57
11:13–15	125n106
11:13	125n105
11:14–15	142
11:14	134
11:18	126n108
11:22	57
11:23	57
11:26	142
12:7	134, 142
12:11	125n105
12:12	57
12:16	57

Galatians

1:6–7	126n112
1:7	142
2:4	142
3:1–3	126n113
3:1	142
4:9	126n114
5:1	126n115
5:7	8

Ephesians

1:21	138
2:2–3	142
2:2	135

3:10	138	1:9	126n122
4:14	121n9, 142	1:15–20	61
4:27	135	1:16	138
5:1	125n102	2:2	126n123
5:6	142	2:3	126n122
5:23–25	121n13	2:4	143
6:10–18	xiii, 32, 126n116	2:6	130n226
		2:8–23	126n125
6:10–12	22	2:8	61, 143
6:11	135, 143	2:10	126n126
6:12	138, 143	2:15	138
6:13	123n41–42	2:16–23	143
6:14–17	23	3:10	126n123
6:16	76	4:2	33, 123n52, n57
6:17	124n61		
6:18	31, 33, 123n51–52	4:3–4	123n58
6:19–20	123n58	**1 Thessalonians**	
		1:6	62, 125n102, 126n128
Philippians		1:7	126n129
1:7	130n216	2:2	62, 126n133
1:13–14	130n216	2:13	126n130
1:15–17	60	2:14–15	62
1:15	126n119, 143	2:14	125n102, 126n128, n134
1:17	126n119, 130n216, 143	2:16	63, 126n135
1:27	126n117	2:18	135
1:28	126n118	3:3–4	62
2:2	126n117	3:4	126n133
2:14	126n117	3:5	135
2:25	130n234	3:7	62
3:2–3	143	5:1–11	29, 31, 123n52
3:2	126n118	5:6	33
3:17	125n102	5:7–8	123n59
3:18–19	143	5:8	32, 124n61
3:18	126n118	5:9	32
4:2	126n117	5:15	126n132
4:6	130n220		
4:13	121n14		
4:14–19	130n233	**2 Thessalonians**	
		1:4–5	126n136
Colossians		1:5–10	63
1:6	130n232	2:3	143

Scripture Index

2 Thessalonians (*continued*)

2:9	135
2:10	143
2:15	126n137
3:2	135
3:7	125n102
3:9	125n102
5:15	126n138

1 Timothy

1:3–7	127n139
1:3	144
1:4	127n141, n159
1:6	127n141
1:7	127n143, n151
1:16	127n148
1:18–19	127n146
1:19	127n145
1:20	135
2:2	127n147–48
2:9–10	127n148
2:10	127n147
2:14	6, 135
3:1–13	122n30
3:2–16	127n148
3:6–7	135
3:16	127n147
4:1–2	144
4:1	127n145, 138
4:7	127n147
4:8	127n147
4:12	127n148
4:15	127n148
5:4–10	127n148
5:8	122n23
5:13–15	127n160
5:15	135
5:25	127n148
6:1–2	127n148
6:3–5	144
6:3–4	127n139
6:3	127n144, n147
6:4	127n141, n143, n157
6:5	127n147, n152
6:6	127n147
6:10	127n145
6:11	127n147
6:12	127n146, n148
6:20–21	127n139
6:20	127n141–42, n158
6:21	127n145

2 Timothy

1:13	125n102, 127n164
1:14	127n165
1:15	127n163
2:1	127n166
2:2–6	127n167
2:3	130n234
2:14	127n157
2:15	127n168
2:16–18	144
2:16	127n158
2:17	127n163
2:22	127n169
2:23	66, 127n159
2:26	135
3:1–5	144
3:6	127n160
3:13	144
3:14	128n170
4:3–4	121n8, 144
4:5	128n171
4:10	127n163
4:12	65
4:16	127n163

Titus

1:1	127n153
1:5	127n149
1:10–16	145
1:10	127n150–51

1:11	127n152	1:23	132n288
1:14	127n150–51	2:17	122n22
1:16	127n154–55	2:19	124n85, 138
2:7	127n154	3:15	138
2:12	127n153	4:4	145
2:14	127n154	4:7	135
3:1	127n154		
3:3	145	**1 Peter**	
3:8	127n154	1:1	128n177
3:9	127n150–51	3:22	138
3:12	65	4:12–14	70
3:14	127n154, n156	5:4	128n178
		5:7	128n179, 130n217
Philemon		5:8–10	71
1	67, 128n172–73	5:8	33, 123n52–53, 131n250, 135, 145
2	130n234		
9–10	128n172	**2 Peter**	
13	128n172	2:1–22	145
16	67	2:12	145
17	67	3:16	146
23	128n172	3:17	146
Hebrews		**1 John**	
2:14	135	2:13	136
4:12	145	2:18	146
5:12–6:1	7	2:22	146
6:1–6	145	2:26	146
10:26–39	145	3:7	146
11	50	3:8	136
11:1	125n88	3:10	136
11:6	53	3:12	136
11:13	51	4:1	146
11:35–38	51	4:3	146
11:39–40	125n90	4:4	136
12:1	121n11, 125n87	5:18–19	136
12:2	124n73		
13:9	145	**2 John**	
		7–10	146
James		7–9	146
1:22	121n10, 124n86		

3 John

3	146
10–11	146
12	146

Jude

4	147
9	136
16	147

Revelation

2:1–3:22	10, 13, 19, 147
2:1–7	9–10, 147
2:8–11	10, 147
2:9	136
2:10	136
2:12–17	10, 147
2:13	136
2:18–29	10, 147
2:24	136
3:1–6	10, 147
3:7–13	10
3:9	136
3:14–22	10, 147
9:20	139
12:9	5, 136, 147
12:10	136
12:12	136
13:16–17	147
16:13–14	147
16:13	139
16:14	139
18:2	139
19:20	147
20:2–3	5, 136, 147
20:2	136
20:7–8	147
20:7	136
20:10	136, 147
21:8	147
22:15	147